FINDING GOD IN THE MARGINS

THE BOOK OF RUTH

Other titles in the Transformative Word series:

The Universal Story: Genesis 1–11
by Dru Johnson

Freed to Be God's Family: The Book of Exodus
by Mark R. Glanville

Deserting the King: The Book of Judges
by David J. H. Beldman

Glimpsing the Mystery: The Book of Daniel
by Barbara M. Leung Lai

God behind the Scenes: The Book of Esther
by Wayne K. Barkhuizen

When You Want to Yell at God: The Book of Job
by Craig G. Bartholomew

Faith amid the Ruins: The Book of Habakkuk
by Heath A. Thomas

Revealing the Heart of Prayer: The Gospel of Luke
by Craig G. Bartholomew

Together for the World: The Book of Acts
by Michael R. Wagenman

Cutting Ties with Darkness: 2 Corinthians
by John D. Barry

Living Doctrine: The Book of Titus
by Daniel L. Akin

Christ Above All: The Book of Hebrews
by Adrio König

Between the Cross and the Throne: The Book of Revelation
by Matthew Y. Emerson

FINDING GOD IN THE MARGINS

THE BOOK OF RUTH

TRANSFORMATIVE WORD

CAROLYN CUSTIS JAMES

Series Editor
Craig G. Bartholomew

St. George's Centre

Finding God in the Margins: The Book of Ruth
Transformative Word

Lexham Press, 1313 Commercial St., Bellingham, WA 98225
LexhamPress.com

St. George's Centre
4691 Palladium Way, Burlington, ON L7M 0W9, Canada
stgeorgesonline.com/centre/

Print: 9781683590804
Digital: 9781683590811

Lexham Editorial Team: Douglas Mangum, Claire Brubaker, and Danielle Thevenaz
Cover Design: Brittany Schrock
Typesetting: ProjectLuz.com

Those with keen eyes to see into the Bible's many richnesses are able to discover the depths of our humanity surrounded by the deep wells of God's grace. *Finding God in the Margins* is not for the faint of heart: this book will sideswipe you with admonishment when you least expect it and then turn a word of grace into redemption.

—Scot McKnight, Julius R. Mantey Professor of New Testament, Northern Seminary, Lisle IL

Every once in awhile I open a book that surprises me with its freshness. I know the story of Ruth, but not the way Carolyn knows it. As a result, there is an "'aliveness"' in the way she frames this story that forces me to be thoughtful and prayerful as I reconsider its rich and deep meaning for my life. This is a story of way back when, but also a story ripe with meaning for today.

—Anita Lustrea, Faith Conversations podcaster, speaker, author, spiritual director

Finding God in the Margins proved to be an edge-of-your-seat gem that will keep you turning pages from start to finish, uncovering God's love throughout.

—Diane Paddison, founder, 4wordwomen.org; author, *Work, Love, Pray* and *Be Refreshed*

Theologically sound and sociologically sensitive, James offers a commentary on the book of Ruth that any pastor could use with integrity in their preaching and teaching. At the same time, James does not shy away from tackling difficult topics and issues. She engages these issues not through rabid rhetoric but through intellectually thoughtful and biblically–rooted reasoning.

—Soong-Chan Rah, Milton B. Engebretson Professor, North Park Theological Seminary; author, *The Next Evangelicalism* and *Prophetic Lament*

Throughout *Finding God in the Margins,* James champions the theme for which she is well-known, showing again and again how the biblical text subverts rather than promotes patriarchy, and calling men and women to a *Blessed Alliance* that pushes against the curse. In reading, I came away with new hope for our embattled world, greater courage in the face of uncertainty, and stronger resolve to remember the lessons of Ruth as I work out my own calling before the God who delivers.

—Matthew Vos, professor of sociology, Covenant College

Carolyn Custis James is a masterful storyteller. Her examination of Naomi, Ruth, and Boaz offers encouragement and comfort to those who are grieving, marginalized, and oppressed, within the dynamics of power and privilege. *Finding God in the Margins: The Book of Ruth* will serve well as a thought-provoking Bible-study or devotional companion reading.

—Ingrid Faro, director of masters programs; affiliate professor of Old Testament, Trinity Evangelical Divinity School

Finding God in the Margins challenges our presuppositions and broadens our horizons. We meet Naomi, Ruth, and Boaz as if for the first time and, more importantly, we discover profound theological truths about a God who meets both them and us in times of crisis.

—Jared E. Alcántara, associate professor of homiletics, Trinity Evangelical Divinity School; author, *Crossover Preaching*

In *Finding God in the Margins*, James offers both women and men timely guidance for understanding and then living out the world-changing love of God. I call this guidance timely because rarely—in my lifetime, at least—has our human inability to love been so evident. And timely, too, because now as then, both the church and secular culture are desperate for hard-earned, practical, transformative wisdom from the margin—from those who have suffered the catastrophes of racism, sexism, displacement, poverty and injustice of any kind. I'm grateful for the scholarship and the passion woven together in this book—and for the woman who has dedicated her life and work to speaking the truths that God-loving women and men need to hear.

—Lynne Hybels, advocate for global engagement, Willow Creek Community Church

Finding God In The Margins expresses God's radical mercy, compassion, and courage through the lives of women and men who accomplish great things together in the Lord. Carolyn Custis James prophetically challenges the patriarchy that devastates and oppresses women, girls, men, and boys throughout the ages and calls us to give ourselves to those on the margins, where we will find God.

—Dr. Paul Louis Metzger, director of The Institute for Cultural Engagement, Multnomah University and Biblical Seminary; author, *Consuming Jesus: Beyond Race and Class Divisions in a Consumer Church*

This engaging, insightful book gives the beloved book of Ruth a fresh voice, a voice about three people inhabiting the margins in the past who experienced God's wonderful, decisive work there. This is just the book to get people talking about Naomi ("the female Job"), Ruth, and Boaz as pointers toward God's gracious, hope-inspiring, kingdom-advancing work in our conflicted context.

—Robert L. Hubbard, Jr., professor emeritus of Old Testament, North Park Theological Seminary, Chicago; general editor of the New International Commentary on the Old Testament series

In *Finding God in the Margins*, Carolyn Custis James delves into the hard reality of the ancient Israelite world to highlight themes in the book of Ruth that are often ignored—namely the gritty, Job-like character of Naomi. The sacrificial love from people around Naomi indirectly answer her pleading questions about God's concern for the marginalized. Carolyn Custis James does not permit Naomi's struggle and lament to be forgotten.

—Cyndi Parker, Clarke Assistant Professor of Biblical Studies, Biblical Theological Seminary, Hatfield, PA

I first really got to know Ruth in Carolyn Custis James' *The Gospel of Ruth*, and I loved her courage. But in *Finding God in the Margins* Carolyn has taken me deeper with Ruth, into the world of refugees, the destitute, total loss, the hopeless. I feel like Ruth has become a model, a mentor, a friend, a hero as she lived out her faith and courage against staggering obstacles. Thank you, God, for creating this woman, and thank you, Carolyn, for helping us to know her. May I live out such faith and courage.

—Judy Douglass, writer; speaker; spiritual arsonist; director, Women's Resources, Cru

TABLE OF CONTENTS

TABLE OF CONTENTS

1

INTRODUCTION

One of the biggest fears in today's world is that something as harmless looking as a backpack will slip undetected through security checks, past bomb-sniffing dogs, and into a crowded area, where it will explode.

That fear became reality—twice—on April 15, 2013, in Boston. On that fateful day during the Boston Marathon, two brothers deposited backpacks 210 feet apart near the finish line in the midst of a preoccupied, cheering crowd. The backpacks contained pressure cookers packed with deadly explosive material that, as planned, exploded sequentially in two devastating blasts.

For Boston, nothing will ever be the same.

Ironically, though the aim of that life-altering attack was to terrorize and disable the community, in the aftermath Bostonians came together. Instead of being paralyzed by fear, the rallying cry resounding in a packed Fenway Park, on Boston city streets, and echoing defiantly round the world was "Boston Strong!"

Overview

It may seem odd to compare the Old Testament book of Ruth to a backpack containing powerful explosives, but for far too long the Christian church has underestimated the potency of this harmless looking ancient narrative.

Traditional interpretations see the book of Ruth as a beautiful love story between the impoverished Moabitess for whom the book is named and Boaz, the wealthy Israelite landowner. It's the kind of story that is suitable for bedtime reading—not to make it hard to sleep at night. The romance interpretation is understandable, given that the story line focuses on the fortuitous meeting between a man (Boaz) and a woman (Ruth). But this is not a Disney movie.

A series of tragic events that befall Ruth's mother-in-law, Naomi and push both Naomi and Ruth over the poverty line serve to draw Boaz and Ruth together. Their meeting ultimately leads to a marriage proposal (unexpectedly coming from Ruth), a wedding, the birth of a son, and, so it seems, to the restoration of the distraught Naomi's spirits. According to this interpretation, the biblical camera settles on Boaz as the hero of the story—a man possessed of wealth, resources, and generosity that reverse the sagging fortunes of the two women.

The story line is all too familiar—seen in countless fairytales and chick flicks (with the possible exception that the man in question usually makes the proposal). The problem comes with preaching a story that has a "happily-ever-after" banner waving over the ending to a congregation living in real-world stories that don't play out like that. Subsequently, the book of Ruth becomes a source of pleasure but doesn't give the reader's faith much substance to grasp.

Perhaps the most significant recent scholarly insight regarding the book of Ruth has been the general consensus that *we are looking at the story of a female Job.*[1] Naomi's losses are catastrophic and pivotal to the story. As we will see, according to ancient patriarchal calculations, Naomi's losses amount to total devastation and raise disturbing questions about God's character that the story will address. The opening five verses describe a devastating litany of tragedies that leave the Israelite Naomi emptied of everything that gave her life meaning.

Parallels between the book of Ruth and the book of Job are striking and further corroborate this interpretation. Both sufferers' losses are catastrophic. Job loses his livestock, servants, children, and his health. Naomi endures famine, the life of a refugee, and the deaths of her husband and both her sons (Job 1:13–2:10; Ruth 1:1–5). It is a total wipeout for both sufferers, the only difference being that Job, as a man in a patriarchal culture, can eventually begin again. Not so Naomi, who, as a postmenopausal widow, is finished.

Both sufferers turn their attention away from secondary causes to YHWH and cry out in protest over the injustices involved in the suffering that God has unleashed on them (Ruth 1:13b, 20–21; Job 6:4; 7:11). Job questions God's justice; Naomi doubts his love (*hesed*). That one word lies at the heart of this story and is the driving force of the action that takes place. (More about that later.) Both are met by friends who find the toll of sorrow has rendered these sufferers unrecognizable (Ruth 1:19; Job 2:11–13). And although in both stories God responds to each in ways that fortify their faith in him in powerful ways, he doesn't explain the reasons behind their losses.

Where the book of Ruth lands in the Bible is significant. In the Jewish Bible, the book of Ruth is located after the book of Proverbs as a beautiful example of wisdom living, a.k.a. living in the fear of God. In the Christian Bible, Ruth follows the book of Judges and precedes 1 Samuel. Viewed at the *macro level*, this narrative forms a sturdy bridge between the "years when the judges ruled" (Ruth 1:1) and the monarchy of King David (4:18–22). At the *micro level* the story centers on urgent family issues and Ruth's reinterpretation of three Mosaic laws: gleaning, levirate, and kinsman-redeemer. Ruth lives on the hungry side of the law, so her perspective differs dramatically from Boaz's. His willingness to listen to her (which is one of the jaw-dropping aspects of this story) moves him from the letter to the spirit of the law. As a result, a hungry widow is fed, and a dying family is rescued.

The original readers of the book of Ruth and people living at that time would notice what is happening in this story at both macro and micro levels. But a third, *cosmic level* is only recognizable from the vantage point of the New Testament and beyond, for God is working through the lives of ordinary and socially insignificant individuals to advance his purposes for the world.

Framing the book of Ruth as a Job story brings this ancient narrative into the twenty-first century. Suddenly this is a story about the real world in which we live, where trouble often strikes unexpectedly and the God who has the power to prevent our sorrows doesn't stop it. Naomi is voicing questions that come to us all. Suddenly her story and her questions belong

OUTLINE

1. Famine drives Naomi's family from Bethlehem to Moab, where her world unravels (1:1–5)
2. Naomi and Ruth return from Moab to Bethlehem (1:6–22)
   a. Naomi's first attempt to send Orpah and Ruth back (1:6–10)
   b. Naomi's second attempt, her lament, and Orpah's return (1:11–14)
   c. Naomi's third attempt, and Ruth's conversion and vow (1:15–18)
   d. Naomi and Ruth arrive in Bethlehem (1:19–22)
3. Ruth advocates for Naomi in the field of Boaz (2:1–23)
   a. Introducing Boaz (2:1)
   b. Ruth decides to glean (2:2–3)
   c. Ruth moves Boaz from the letter to the spirit of the gleaning law (2:4–17)
   d. Ruth returns to Naomi, whose hope in YHWH's *hesed* revives (2:18–23)
4. Ruth advocates for Naomi at the threshing floor (3:1–18)
   a. Naomi seeks rest (security) for Ruth (3:1–5)
   b. Ruth seeks a male heir to rescue the family of Naomi and Elimelech (3:6–9)
   c. Boaz reveals a nearer kinsman-redeemer and vows to fulfill Ruth's proposal (3:10–14)
   d. Ruth returns to Naomi, and Boaz will not rest (3:15–18)
5. Boaz advocates for Naomi at the city gate (4:1–17)
   a. Boaz assembles a quorum of elders (4:1–2)
   b. Boaz presents the sale of Naomi's land to the kinsman-redeemer (4:3–4)
   c. Boaz presents marriage to Ruth as a condition (4:5–8)
   d. The marriage of Ruth and Boaz (4:9–11)
   e. "Naomi has a son!" (4:12–17)
6. A royal genealogy (Ruth 4:18–22)

to us too. We have a stake in how the book of Ruth plays out. The story that follows—the bold initiatives of Ruth and the astonishing responses of Boaz—will take us into uncharted territory, where this harmless looking little story, like the red pill in the Matrix, will awaken us to a whole new world and a whole new way of being human that will reconfigure our lives and leave us longing for more. It will raise the bar for what it means to live in a fallen world as God's child—as his image bearers. It presents a startling vision of the kingdom potency of male/female relationships and will inject rich hope, purpose, and significance into the veins of the most God-forsaken, hollowed-out human soul.

Keys to Unlock the Message of Ruth

Recognizing Naomi as a female Job is the first step in digging deeper into the story. But there is more. As we proceed through the book, four indispensible keys will aid us in getting to the heart of this ancient story.

First, God is always the hero of the story. The primary purpose of the Bible is always to teach us more about him, about his character, his ways, his heart for the world and for us, so that we will trust and love him more and reflect his heart in how we live and interact with others. Ultimately, the book of Ruth is all about God. In Naomi's suffering, God's character is on the line. Rich theology emerges—truth about God that we need to move forward in our own stories. Here we will see God through the eyes of Naomi, Ruth, and Boaz and how their awareness of his love impacts and empowers them. If someone or something else becomes the central focus of the story, we will miss the main point.

Second, this smaller story is framed within God's greater story. The book of Ruth holds a strategic place in the global rescue effort God launched in the garden of Eden when his first two image bearers were making excuses for rebelling and defecting to the Enemy. Devastating as that moment was, God never abandoned his vision for the world he loves. He created a world where human beings—both male and female—would thrive on their relationship with him and would flourish as they joined forces for his purposes. He bestowed jointly on his sons and daughters the exalted privilege of reflecting his character and looking after things in his world. He empowered us to be his eyes, his ears, his hands, and his voice in the world he loves. Image bearing is the highest calling. It comes with the enormous responsibility to speak and act on his behalf. God calls his sons and daughters to do this together as a Blessed Alliance (Gen 1:27–28).[2]

First, this means a relationship with our Creator is our lifeline. Every person's first and highest calling is to know the God we are created to be like. Second, it means the impact of the fall has caused us to lose sight of what God had in mind for us in the beginning. We are living in the ruins of the world he first created, sifting through the rubble for clues that tell us what he has in mind for us, which is why God gave us stories such as the one we are about to study. We need to see examples of the countercultural kingdom way of living that Jesus came to restore. And third, it means image bearing is no spectator sport but a vocation. It is a call to action. What happens in God's world is our business. The three major characters in this story rise up to

BLESSED ALLIANCE

The expression "Blessed Alliance" was first coined by Carolyn Custis James (*Lost Women of the Bible: The Women We Thought We Knew* [Grand Rapids: Zondervan, 2005], 37–38), based on God blessing his male and female image bearers and commissioning them to do his work in the world together.

> "So God created mankind in his image, in the image of God he created them; male and female he created them. *God blessed them* and said to them, 'Be fruitful and increase in number; fill the earth and subdue it. Rule over the fish in the sea and the birds in the sky and over every living creature that moves on the ground.' " (Gen 1:27–28, emphasis added)

Genesis elevates this Blessed Alliance to a kingdom strategy. The alliance is not confined to marriage but encompasses all male/female relations and is ultimately to be reflected in the church as the body of Christ. The book of Ruth provides a powerful example as Ruth, Boaz, and Naomi join forces to address local family problems, but God works through their sacrificial actions for others to advance his purposes for the world.

embrace this high calling. They give us a rare glimpse of the kingdom potency that is unleashed when God's sons and daughters together pour themselves out for his purposes. The beautiful irony is that the three of them never realize the far-reaching global impact of their selfless actions, which were intended merely to address local, family matters.

Third, the Bible is not an American or Western book. Every time we open the Bible we need to remind ourselves of this. As Westerners we study the Bible at a huge disadvantage, for our culture is as far removed from the world of the Bible as we can get in today's world. Without significant outside help, we will distort, diminish, or miss entirely the message of the story. Fortunately, in today's multicultural, globalized world, we are actually rubbing shoulders with people who come from patriarchal cultures and can help us. We need them to educate us to the social realities of a patriarchal society.

The story of Ruth takes place within a full-fledged patriarchal culture. Patriarchy is a social system that privileges men over women, where the actions of men command the focus, and women (with few exceptions) recede into the background. Under patriarchy, a woman derives her value from men—her father, husband, and especially her sons. Sons are patriarchy's gold standard for determining the value of a woman. That standard of measurement has a devastating impact on both Naomi and Ruth, but we will not recognize the magnitude of that impact if we view their story through an American lens and ignore the patriarchal backdrop that intensifies the severity of the crisis they face and the terrible odds stacked against them.

Israel and Moab are the two cultures in which the book of Ruth takes place. *Both* are fallen cultures and *both* are intensely patriarchal. Every narrative in the Bible takes place within this fallen context. This means—whether in their world or in ours—we must be careful to distinguish fallen ways that human beings organize and relate to one another from the world as God created it in the beginning and that Jesus came to restore. Jesus didn't come to give us a kinder, gentler patriarchy or a new-and-improved version of any other social system known to humankind. In his own words, he came to bring a "kingdom that is *not of this world*" (John 18:36, emphasis added)—the kingdom we lost in the fall, a kingdom that is utterly foreign to us.

The mistake we so often make is to assume patriarchy—at least some softer version of it—is the Bible's message for us. But patriarchy is *not* the Bible's message. Rather, it is the cultural backdrop against which the gospel message of Jesus stands out in the sharpest relief.

Making this distinction will enable us to see how the book of Ruth puts on display the inbreaking of the gospel into a fallen culture and how it upends the choices and sacrifices that Ruth, Boaz, and Naomi will make—sacrifices driven by putting the interests of others ahead of themselves instead of capitulating to their culture's way of doing things. Their actions actually subvert the patriarchal value system and practices and point to a gospel way of living as God's image bearers. The book of Ruth is in many ways a critique of patriarchy. According to patriarchal values, both Naomi and Ruth have lost all value and ability to make any meaningful contribution to society. In opposition to that value system, YHWH is raising up both women for significant kingdom purposes. Boaz, in response to Ruth's initiatives, will subvert the very patriarchal mores that most benefit him as a man. Instead, he will sacrificially employ those benefits and privileges to empower Ruth and to benefit Naomi. In the process, he will put on display Jesus' kingdom brand of manhood that is desperately needed in today's world.[3]

Even if you already know the story of Naomi and Ruth, you may be sensing that the drama in this little story will be more intense than previously thought.

Fourth, the Bible is a literary work of art. Writers of the Bible were literary artists and gifted storytellers. They beautifully crafted their stories so that not a single word is wasted. Our English Bibles break the biblical text into chapters and verses in a way that sometimes disrupts the flow of scenes seamlessly presented in the Hebrew story. So we must self-consciously bring all that happens in the first scene into the second, and from the first and second into the third, and so on, if we hope to grasp the beauty of what's happening.

Everything matters and everything holds together.

The story of Ruth takes place in two countries—the village of Bethlehem in Israel and Moab (today's Jordan). Events occur on the connecting road between the two countries, in Naomi's home, at Boaz's field, at his threshing floor, and at Bethlehem's seat of government, the city gate.

Hebrew writers employ a literary tactic most Western readers would find annoying. We prefer variety in wording and don't like hearing the same word repeated over and over. Translators of our English Bibles tend to accommodate us by using different words to translate the same Hebrew word in the original text. So we miss clues ancient writers were dropping to highlight major themes or to alert the reader of the main point of the story. The book of Ruth has several of these repeated words, which I'll point out as we go along.

All three lead characters—Naomi, Ruth, and Boaz—undergo significant character development from the start of the story to the conclusion. God uses their interaction with each other to transform them. Together the three of them create a breathtaking display of the power of Jesus' gospel to transform human lives and relationships centuries before his birth.

Fear or Faith?

As we move steadily into the third millennium, we are more aware than ever of threats to our safety and security. Terrorism, warfare, nuclear arms races, stock-market volatility, globalization, seismic cultural shifts, natural disasters, global warming—it is a time that easily could paralyze us with fear. Changes are happening at warp speed that challenge long-held assumptions and thrust us forward into the unknown. Daily we are confronted with conflicting impulses either to retreat into the so-called safety of the known past or to move forward with hope and courage into the unknown future.

Naomi, Ruth, and Boaz also lived in a tumultuous time. The global stage was dominated by political instability, penetrated national borders, gender inequality, racial disparity, international tensions, economic crises, injustice, violence, wars, and natural disasters. "In the days when the judges ruled" is hardly a propitious beginning.[4] Even without cable news or internet access, all three characters were doubtless regularly bombarded with alarming news. Closer to home, family problems weighed heavily. Economic recovery from an extended famine doesn't happen overnight. In the ancient world, for a family to die without a male heir was a fate most feared. Everyone was struggling. It was a time when a person's problems could easily be unnoticed by others too consumed with their own problems and who otherwise might lend a helping hand.

Into these dire circumstances we enter, with a fresh awareness that all is not right in God's world and hasn't been since the fall of humanity. But it is here—in the mess, amid losses, despair, darkness, and frightening possibilities—that God is marvelously at work in the most unlikely ways through the most unexpected agents. His kingdom can be wonderfully subversive. Here he will reaffirm in unexpected ways his unrelenting love for his daughters and sons. He will demonstrate in fresh, earthshaking ways that he has never wavered from his original creation vision of his sons and daughters ruling and subduing creation on his behalf. He still intends for his image bearers to be agents together who accomplish his good purposes in the world he loves.

Ironically, despite the calamities that fell on the little community in Bethlehem, in the aftermath of famine and loss, God intervened. Two Bethlehemites and one undocumented immigrant came together. Their refusal to be paralyzed by fear meant the story that played out didn't end with "happily-ever-after" but with a courageous "Bethlehem Strong!" as God's kingdom purposes advanced for the world.

So let's get started ...

SUGGESTED READING

- ☐ Ruth 1:1
- ☐ Judges 2:6–19

Reflection

How does viewing the book of Ruth as the story of Naomi, a female Job, contrast with how you've previously viewed the story or heard it taught?

Why do *both* women and men need the story of a female Job?

How does the Job-like nature of this story put God at the center, and why is that crucial in reading and studying any part of the Bible?

What similarities can you see between your world and Naomi's (politically, culturally, religiously)?

2

ENTERING THE WORLD OF NAOMI AND RUTH

The opening lines of the book of Ruth are often the first to get set aside and forgotten once the action in the story gets rolling. But these first eight sentences contain vital information that we must carry with us through the entire story. When probed within the cultural context, these introductory facts not only deepen the pathos of the unfolding drama, but they also open the way for us to begin connecting the dots between Naomi's story and our own.

One of the reasons for leaving this information behind is that Naomi's losses become utilitarian. Calamities she suffers serve to bring Ruth into the story in the first place and into Boaz's life as a now-unmarried young woman and prospective bride. All too often the way Naomi's story is told to us doesn't stir a twinge of sympathy for her. Instead, we've trivialized her suffering and criticized her for complaining. We've even blamed her for her troubles and been impatient for her to "get over it" and move on. We've managed to persuade ourselves that a bit of good luck—a second marriage and a baby for her daughter-in-law Ruth—could cure the ache she felt inside over the deaths of her husband and two sons. Besides that, Naomi isn't the character who interests us. So we reduce her to a sidebar as the story moves forward to the fortuitous meeting between Ruth and Boaz.

In doing so, we sidestep the heart of what the book of Ruth is all about. So it behooves us to pause here in the beginning to look more closely at Naomi and her losses and, more importantly, to view the calamities she suffers through the lens of patriarchy.

Naomi in Context

Two facts about Naomi intensify her losses. First, she is an Israelite—a daughter of YHWH, a descendant of Abraham, and an heir of YHWH's promises of blessing. According to the story, there is reason to believe that at least one of the reasons Naomi's losses provoke such a powerful sense of outrage and injustice in her is the expectation that the payoff for faithfully following God will be being spared the heartaches of life.

We tend to share similar expectations, often fueled by books and sermons that promise a smooth path for those whose lives are upright. Like Naomi, we are blindsided when trouble breaks through anyway—despite faithful living and pleading prayers for God to make it stop. Why is this happening to me? Why doesn't God answer my prayers? Does he really care about me?

Life is profoundly and inescapably theological for those who believe God loves and is looking out for us. Naomi's troubles don't happen in a vacuum, and she will draw a straight line between her losses and YHWH.

So the story is off to a bad start when we read "there was a famine in the land." The anonymous "land" is the land of Palestine that God promised to Abraham and his descendants—a land "flowing with milk and honey" that is instead ravaged by famine. No explanation is given as to what caused the famine. What is clear is that this is the first of a litany of adversities that completely alter Naomi's life and that ultimately will lead her into a crisis of faith.

In any era, "famine" isn't a term that is tossed around lightly. According to the United Nations, in modern times

> a famine can be declared only when certain measures of mortality, malnutrition and hunger are met. They are: at least 20 per cent of households in an area face extreme food shortages with a limited ability to cope; acute malnutrition rates exceed 30 per cent; and the death rate exceeds two persons per day per 10,000 persons.[1]

Those of us in the West who have never experienced a famine or traveled to famine-ravaged regions are left to imagine the frightening scarcity of food or the desperate lengths we would go to if our own children were starving. The famine in the land was so severe that Elimelech (Naomi's husband) packed up his family and left Bethlehem. They migrated to Moab, where there was food.

The hard fact is that Elimelech, Naomi, and their sons, Mahlon and Kilion, were famine refugees. Wrap that cold fact around what we routinely see on cable

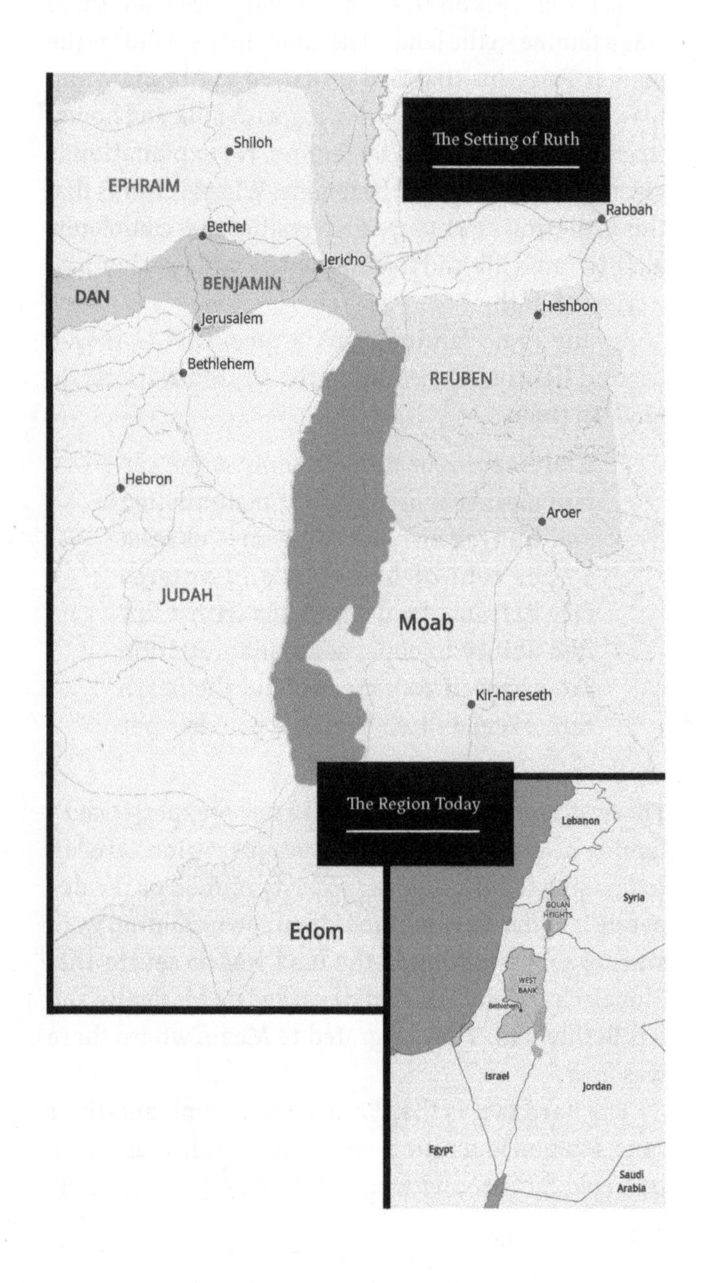
The Setting of Ruth
Shiloh
EPHRAIM
Bethel
Jericho
Rabbah
BENJAMIN
DAN
Jerusalem
Heshbon
Bethlehem
REUBEN
Hebron
Aroer
JUDAH
Moab
Kir-hareseth
Edom
The Region Today
Lebanon
Syria
GOLAN HEIGHTS
WEST BANK
Bethlehem
Israel
Jordan
Egypt
Saudi Arabia

news and the internet of the widespread suffering and misery of refugees. We witness at a distance their suffering. Difficult as it must be to be compelled to flee your homeland because of famine, war, or terrorism, what awaits in refugee camps is often simply exchanging one form of misery for another. We've seen pictures of temporary shelters (such as they are), heard reports of the ongoing challenges concerning food, adequate clothing, disease, cessation of education, and the demoralizing reality that no one knows when this ordeal will end. Worse still to be regarded as "the other"—unwelcome burdens on the locals and targets of mistreatment.

Certainly the life of a famine refugee was never something Naomi envisioned for herself, much less that her exile would last for over a decade. The intended time frame for their time away from home was "for a while." But things don't work according to plan. This one dimension of her suffering ought to wring from us deep empathy and compassion, as it should for refugees today.

There is more.

The second fact that intensifies Naomi's losses is that she is female in a patriarchal world. Already we have noted that, within patriarchy, women (with few exceptions) are ancillary to men, who command the storyline. Naomi derives value from the men in her family. Her primary responsibility as a wife was to produce sons for her husband.

As the mother of two sons, Naomi has successfully fulfilled her duty to her husband, and her value seems secure. Devastating as Elimelech's death must have been for her—especially leaving her stranded as a refugee widow in Moab—her two sons provide the grieving widow with double insurance for her future. Her boys will care for her. They also hold the promise that the family will survive for another generation.

Still, it cannot have been easy for her when her sons intermarried with Moabite girls. No Israelite mother envisions her sons marrying foreign women, and Israelite history provided Naomi with plenty of reasons to fear their pagan influence (e.g., Exod 34:16; Num 25:1–3). Naomi's daughters-in-law were foreigners and worshipers of Chemosh. Generations later, Chemosh is described as "the detestable god of Moab," one of the many gods King Solomon's foreign wives enticed him to worship (1 Kgs 11:1–7).

In the desperate quest for sons, puberty signaled a girl's readiness for marriage. So in biblical times, child marriages would have been the norm. The marriages of Mahlon and Kilion lasted for ten years. The fact that not a single pregnancy is mentioned within those ten years suggests a whole new layer of suffering afflicted this family. Given a woman's normal monthly menstrual cycle, Naomi endured with her daughters-in-law, Ruth and Orpah, as many as 240 increasingly agonizing disappointments.

Although infertility today is a profound heartache, it rose to epic proportions in biblical times. Accounts of the desperation of barren women such as Sarah, Rebekah, Rachel, and Hannah are not overblown. Desperation for sons led them to extremes. Sarah, Rachel, and her sister Leah compelled their slave girls to become surrogates to produce more sons for their mistresses. In today's parlance, we'd call that sex trafficking. Barrenness drove Hannah to make a radical vow—that if YHWH would bless her with a son, she would dedicate him once weaned (meaning a very young child) to the tabernacle. It is telling that these women were only desperate for sons. None of them were begging YHWH to bless them with a daughter.

Welcome to patriarchy.

A Tanzanian friend of mine who grew up in patriarchy explained that in his culture a wife who fails to get pregnant or only gives birth to daughters is in trouble. Her husband will divorce her or he will add a second wife (as Hannah's husband did). Polygamy gives a husband options, for a man must have sons.

After ten years without a single pregnancy between them, both Ruth and Orpah bore the stigma of barrenness. By then, both of Naomi's sons would have been contemplating their options. Yet instead of the long-awaited pregnancy or one or both of Naomi's sons resorting to other means of securing the necessary male heir to carry on the family name, the unspeakable happened—both Mahlon and Kilion died.

The Expiration of Hope

The cumulative effect of Naomi's losses coupled with YHWH's silence created spiritual vertigo for her. The deaths of her sons represent a complete destruction of her life's work. Within the context of the ancient patriarchal culture, the day they buried Mahlon and Kilion, they essentially buried Naomi too.[2] Now past childbearing years, Naomi has no future and no hope. Unlike Job, there is no prospect of starting over for this postmenopausal widow.

Instead, the future promises her more troubles. The deaths of all the men in the family instantly put Naomi and her daughters-in-law at risk. On their own in the ancient culture, unprotected widows became targets for abuse, exploitation, assault, and even trafficking. Under patriarchy women have no independent legal rights and no voice. Rights and protections women in the West naturally assume are completely absent for Naomi and her daughters-in-law. Anyone can abuse them with impunity, since there is no male to defend them against an assailant. Their future is frightening—promising only poverty, vulnerability, and misery.

The book of Ruth turns a spotlight on the plight of women in the world for the whole church to learn. This issue started at the fall and has escalated down through the ages to the present. In their 2009 New York Times bestseller, *Half the Sky: Turning Oppression into Opportunity for Women Worldwide*, authors Nicholas Kristof and Sheryl WuDunn expose systemic human rights violations against women and girls globally. Their research includes such human rights violations against women and girls as sex trafficking, honor killings, female genital mutilation, banning education for girls, child marriages, female gendercide, and rape as a weapon of war. In blunt terms and without overstating their case, Kristof and WuDunn describe the significance of this issue today as "the paramount moral challenge of the twenty-first century."[3]

The book of Ruth provides us with an opportunity to engage this crisis, if we have eyes to see it. But seeing it means looking at their story through a different lens. We must delve deeper into the patriarchal world for women.

The Value of a Woman

The book of Ruth also raises the subject of the value of a woman—a question that patriarchy answers without blinking. What is Naomi worth? Count her sons. According to that cultural scorecard, Naomi is a zero. So is her barren daughter-in-law Ruth. But is that how God sees them? Is a woman's value truly derived from others? Or is it grounded in something that can never change? Death and childlessness severed these widows from anything that gave them meaning or value. When the last man in the family died, they both plummeted to the bottom of the social ladder—whether they lived in Moab or Israel.

No one would feel that more profoundly than the women themselves.

In today's world, "It's a girl!" are three of the most dangerous words uttered in cultures where patriarchal values are in full force. To be sure, there are striking examples of parents in those cultures whose hearts are just as captivated by their daughters as by their sons. But they are the exception, not the norm, in cultures that place a premium on sons over daughters. A son will build his father's name and estate. But a daughter will marry and build another man's family.

A woman who worked as an obstetrical nurse in India observed those values in action. She described the dramatic difference between what happened when a woman gave birth to a son versus a daughter. When a son was born, the news was greeted with noisy, jubilant celebration. In contrast, the birth of a daughter was met with silence. She expressed distress over how difficult it often was to persuade a mother to hold her newborn daughter. Often the bride who fails to produce a son will experience abuse at the hands of her husband and in-laws.

Naomi's catastrophic losses complete the collapse of her world. We find her sitting in the smoldering ruins of the life she once knew with no hope of recovery. She has no choice but to buy into the culture's view of her. Anyone in Naomi's world—including Naomi herself—would tell us with absolute certainty, "The story is over." Who cares about two women who are zeros? Once the men are wiped from the story, there is no story.

This is where the Bible begs to differ with the world's way of devaluing women. For it is at this point that, much to our surprise, the biblical camera zooms in on two childless women—two zeros—and the real story begins.

The plight of women is front and center, but so is the Bible's radically different view of women and their value in God's eyes. So how do these women move forward into a future that is as grim as possible and in which their prospects match their numeric value—zero?

SUGGESTED READING

- ☐ Ruth 1:1–5
- ☐ Isaiah 1:17, 23; 10:1–2
- ☐ Mark 12:38–40
- ☐ Luke 20:45–47

Reflection

How do reports of refugees in today's world shed light on Naomi's experience with famine and living as a refugee?

How did her life unravel in Moab? How was she now at risk?

As they will for Naomi, how do your own struggles and losses shape your view of God?

Why are these struggles important?

3

INCONSOLABLE

For many refugees, if they have any dreams at all, their only dream is of returning to their homeland. However deep those longings may be, thoughts of returning home inevitably are a cauldron of mixed feelings—a sense of relief at the prospect of home, of the familiar, of shedding the "foreigner" label, and of belonging, accompanied by uncertainty and dread at what "home" will look like, who will be missing, and how much of their former life will be destroyed.

So far, the twenty-first century has been a gut-wrenching education on what life is like for refugees. Terrorism, bombings, civil wars, and the accompanying threat of starvation as food supplies are cut off have driven millions of refugees away from home in a desperate, often fatal quest for sanctuary. Whole cities have been reduced to rubble. Communities have been dismantled. Civilian casualties are in the hundreds of thousands. Countless relatives, friends, and neighbors are gone forever. The Mediterranean Sea has become a watery graveyard of thousands of unmarked graves—fleeing refugee families packed into overcrowded smuggler boats that never made it to European shores. The world was aghast and sympathies soared (at least momentarily) when photos went viral of three-year-old Syrian refugee toddler Aylan Kurdi's tiny lifeless body washed up on the shore of the Mediterranean Sea.[1]

Naomi's decision to return to Bethlehem was prompted by news that the famine in Bethlehem was finally over. YHWH "had come to the aid of his people by providing food for them" (1:6). She wasn't returning to a bombed-out village but to a famine-stricken community in recovery. Bethlehem was once again living up to its name—the "house of bread."

Even so, the Bethlehem to which Naomi was returning bore no resemblance to the Bethlehem she once knew. The place would be full of holes. That's even how she saw herself. She said as much when she described herself as "empty" (1:21), hollowed out, drained of all that once gave her value and meaning. The old life she enjoyed along with every tender hope for the future lay buried back in Moab. Every familiar place in Bethlehem would stir up memories and stabbing reminders that Elimelech and her boys were no more. Death cruelly cheated her of the joys of motherhood and the honor due a mother of two sons. Living out her days back in the country she called home might in some ways be an improvement over her refugee ordeal in Moab, but this final chapter of her story promised nothing more than running out the clock. Naomi was going home—not to live again but to die.

Widows in India today, cast out on the streets to the life of a beggar by families who regard them as encumbrances, speak for Naomi. "This is not life. We all died the day our husbands died. How can anyone describe our pain? Our hearts are all on fire with sorrow. Now we just wait for the day when all this will end."[2]

The Ties That Bind

It is important to note that, in patriarchal cultures, families (usually fathers) negotiate marriages with the intention of cementing beneficial alliances with other families that will enhance the family's stature in the community. Already we have seen how these marriages would have been objectionable to Naomi from a spiritual point of view. But from a Moabite point of view, these unions would have reflected poorly on the brides of Naomi's sons, whose fathers were willing to marry them off to famine refugees. Famine refugees offered *nothing* of benefit—no status, property, or wealth—to enhance the standing of the brides' families, which was the whole point of marriage negotiations. That's called marrying down.

Contrary to the explicit biblical instruction for a man to leave his father and mother and to unite as one with his wife (Gen 2:24), within patriarchy even today a bride is absorbed into her husband's family. She comes under enormous pressure to produce a male heir and is often responsible to serve her in-laws. But marriage is a financial transaction where money (the bride price) changes hands, and the bride becomes the property of her husband's family.

We don't know how the marriages of Naomi's sons came about, but it is evident from what happens next that, even though their husbands were dead, both young women remained bound to Naomi. It is an arrangement she intends to change, not because she doesn't love or need them but because she is determined to spare them from the empty life, suffering, and danger that await them in Bethlehem.

It seems likely that Naomi waited until they were en route to Bethlehem before revealing her plan, reasoning that if she raised the matter while they were still in Moab, the girls might have prevailed on her to stay. Her decision to emancipate them is the first sacrificial act of compassion in the story. Given Naomi's distressed state of mind and despair of the future, it is breathtakingly gospel, to say the least, that she has the presence of mind to put their interests ahead of her own.

Crisis on the Road to Bethlehem

Naomi's decision to send Ruth and Orpah back to Moab is straightforward and makes perfect sense. When Naomi stops abruptly and, with gentle words of gratitude and blessing, instructs her daughters-in-law to return to their mother's home, the pros of returning to Moab far outweigh the cons of continuing on to Bethlehem. "Go back, each of you, to your mother's home. May the Lord show you kindness, as you have shown kindness to your dead husbands and to me. May the Lord grant that each of you will find rest in the home of another husband" (1:8).

Any future—any "rest"—for the two young women hinged on reintegrating in society via a second marriage. Prospects for marriage in Bethlehem would be nil for a pagan gentile girl who was certifiably barren. Moab meant home, family, and male protection, and the possibility of a second marriage. Even so, after ten years of marriage and no child to show for it, the best they could hope was to become an extra pair of hands in a polygamous marriage as wife number two or three. No sensible man who took seriously his duty to father a son for the family would accept a barren wife under any other terms. But at least that would bring Ruth and Orpah under the shelter of a male umbrella.

Loud weeping follows Naomi's instructions, along with her daughter-in-law's united insistence in going on with her to Bethlehem. Naomi is undeterred.

Her second attempt is more forceful. She will make them understand the dire realities of life in Bethlehem. In Western cultures today, widows (even elderly widows) remarry and begin a fresh chapter of their lives. Younger widows often have careers or rejoin the workforce. Many are financially secure already or benefit from life insurance policies. In ancient Israelite culture, with rare exceptions, lone widows resided at the bottom of the social ladder and were instantly at risk. Their vulnerability was exacerbated because they wore garments that identified them as widows (Gen 38:14).[3]

Naomi isn't testing the loyalty or love of her daughters-in-law when she insists they turn back to Moab. She is acting in their best interest and sparing them the rough road ahead—a longer road for them if, according to normal life expectancy, they outlive her and are utterly stranded and even more at risk as immigrants.

So she spells out in the starkest terms the hopeless future they would face in Bethlehem. The center of her argument is the levirate law—a legal safety net the Mosaic law provided when a man died without a son. This family law was in practice within patriarchy long before the exodus and is also found in other cultures.[4] The law stipulated that if a man died without a son, his blood brother was to marry his widow. The first son born of that union would take the dead man's place on the family tree.[5] The levirate law comes up again later in the story, where we'll explore it in more detail. But the point Naomi is making at the moment is, first, that she, the widow in question whose dead husband now has no living male heir, is past childbearing years. If by some miraculous event, she married that very night and conceived male twins, it was absurd to think Orpah and Ruth would wait for those babies to reach marriageable age. But the law in their case was moot anyway because Naomi was postmenopausal. The road ahead involved marginalization and exclusion, a frightening vulnerability, poverty, and hunger, and no hope for pagan, gentile, barren women to reenter the marriage market. Naomi knows the realities and has firsthand experience of living in a foreign culture. All this makes returning to Moab all the more compelling, especially when by returning to Moab they would at least have some hope of marriage.

It also had another effect.

THE DESPERATE QUEST FOR SONS

Throughout history in cultures where patriarchal values prevail, intolerable shame and rejection descend on the wife who fails to produce the required male heir. Both husbands and in-laws are known to punish a childless bride, sometimes in vicious, life-threatening ways. Yet according to medical studies, causes of infertility are shared equally between the woman and the man, and scientists in the early twentieth century proved that the father's X and Y chromosomes determines a child's sex, not the mother's. Who knows how many women have been condemned and punished for a "crime" they didn't commit?[6]

The Dark Night of the Soul

It is as if by verbalizing the grim realities of her circumstances and future, a dam suddenly bursts, as a torrent of grief washes over Naomi. Suddenly her suffering finds theological expression as she raises her voice in lament over the ultimate loss. "No my daughters. It is more bitter for me than for you, because the LORD's hand has turned against me" (1:13b).

Even though at this point the decibel of pathos begins escalating, it is crucial to freeze the action here and focus on what is happening with Naomi as she draws a straight line between her catastrophic losses and YHWH. She sees YHWH as the ultimate source of her trouble. This is the moment when Naomi's critics mobilize. They take her to task for being angry at God for her losses. They scold her for accusing him of raising his hand against her. They criticize her for bitterness. Surely a woman of faith would reach out in faith and have something more inspiring to say, especially in front of her unbelieving daughters-in-law.

Instead, we are witnessing a Job moment—where Naomi speaks what is in her heart in words that mirror Job's, who spoke as candidly, "[YHWH] has made me his target; his archers surround me. ... The Almighty, who has made me taste bitterness of soul" (Job 16:12–13; 27:2).

The stories and honest laments of both sufferers are in the Bible because they are instructive for us. First, they open the door for us to be honest with God, who already knows what we're thinking and feeling. We cannot have a real relationship if honesty doesn't lie at the core. In the Bible there are more lament psalms than any other kind of psalm. All too often it is impossible for us to piece together the God who loves us with the tragedies that invade our stories and the stories of those we love. It's even hard to hear news reports of the suffering of people we don't know without those "why?" questions bubbling to the surface. According to the Bible, such questions are not just permissible; they are important. Naomi and Job aren't the only believers in Scripture who get angry and wrestle with God. Trouble has a way of riveting our focus on God with painful questions that won't go away. Naomi's pain and the questions that result lie at the heart of the book of Ruth.

Naomi is a true believer, a lifelong follower of YHWH, a daughter of Abraham who is heir to the promises of God. She isn't consumed with introspective questions about whether she or someone in the family did something wrong to bring all this disaster on her. She only suspects a further loss—that she has lost God's love for her. Why would he care about an empty old woman whose life is over?

The rest of the story is the response to Naomi's challenge. Just as for Job, YHWH will not answer Naomi's questions or explain why she suffered so much tragedy. But her struggle will take her to a deeper understanding of his heart for her. We need Naomi's struggle and pain. We need Naomi. We need her lament. We need her doubt of God's love, for inevitably we will cry out ourselves or need to sit with someone who is angry and doubting and be able to let them vent their true thoughts.

Her cries of despair make what happens next all the more remarkable.

SUGGESTED READING

- ☐ Ruth 1:6–13
- ☐ Job 27:2–4
- ☐ Jeremiah 3:12–13
- ☐ Psalm 13

Reflection

How would you compare Naomi and Job? How are they different?

___

___

___

What would a childless widow like Naomi's future prospects be in a patriarchal culture compared to her prospects in the contemporary West?

___

___

___

How does this underscore the problem of viewing the Bible through American eyes instead of through the lens of the ancient patriarchal culture?

How does Naomi's honesty invite you to be honest with God about your grief, doubts, and anger?

4

UNDOCUMENTED!

United States history is largely the story of immigrants. Unless you are Native American (a descendant of America's original residents) or were brought here against your will as a slave (African Americans and people trafficked here today for sex or forced labor), what got you here in the first place can be traced to immigrants.

The first Europeans to set foot on American soil didn't travel here on a round-trip ticket. They came to stay. Since then, immigrants have arrived to America's open doors from virtually every country in the world. More than two hundred years later, it appears that immigrants are nation builders. The Statue of Liberty is a monument to America's welcome to immigrants.

During the 2016 presidential election, it became clear that attitudes toward immigrants have changed. During and after the campaign, immigrants were at the center of an intense political storm. Fears among U.S. citizens of foreign terrorists and a deepening suspicion of "the other" escalated, stoked by caricatures of immigrants as criminals, possible terrorists sneaking in under the guise of being refugees, and resentment that immigrants are taking jobs and benefiting from

US welfare, medical care, and education. The US welcome mat got pulled in and was replaced by talk of bans, walls, and mass deportation.

"Undocumented" immigrants became especially vulnerable. Having arrived in the states covertly and without the proper immigration papers and process, they became the focus of deportation. Fears that once gripped American citizens were transferred to America's immigrant population, many of whom have been here for decades, have worked hard, contributed to the economy, and whose totally American children—either born here or brought over the border as minors—have only memories of life in the United States.

Immigrants in the Bible

Biblical history is largely the story of immigrants too. God called Abraham to become an immigrant, moving him from Iraq (Ur) to Turkey (Haran) and finally into Palestine (Canaan; Gen 12:1, 4–5). His grandson Jacob and Jacob's sons (the fathers of Israel's twelve tribes) became immigrants in Egypt during a severe regional famine (Gen 46:1–27). They never left.

Four hundred and thirty years and multiple generations later (Exod 12:40), Moses and Joshua led a whole nation of immigrants (Jacob's descendants) on a forty-year journey from Egypt back to Palestine, where they settled. Mosaic law contains numerous strong instructions regarding immigrants (a.k.a. "the foreigner") in Israel and how YHWH expected Israelites to care for them (Exod 22:21; 23:9, 12; Lev 23:22; Deut 10:18–19). "When a foreigner resides among you in your land, do not mistreat them. The foreigner residing among you must be treated as your native-born. Love them as yourself, for you were foreigners in Egypt. I am the LORD your God" (Lev 19:33–34).

Old Testament prophets preached stinging messages decrying the injustices done to immigrants within Israel's borders (Jer 7:6; 22:3; Ezek 22:7, 29; Mal 3:5). And Jesus, of course, didn't perform miracles just for Israelites but also for foreigners.

Push and Pull

The young immigrant who is the focus of our study came from Jordan (Moab). If Ruth's story took place today, she'd be classified as Arab and most likely be a Muslim. Despite all that, she crossed the border from Jordan into Israel without a hitch. There was no ban on Jordanians, no security checkpoint, no wall or barbed-wire fences, no drones or border patrol. Not even extreme vetting. It was a good thing because she didn't have a passport, visa, or green card.

One might say she was "undocumented."

Researchers studying immigration patterns developed a theory that describes why people immigrate in terms of "push" and "pull" factors.[1] *Push* factors are whatever drives a person to leave their homeland—forces such as famine, violence, warfare, persecution, and poverty. *Pull* factors draw them to a particular country—proximity, a warmer climate, more affordable economy, education, jobs, political asylum, and uniting with relatives already there.

A 2012 Gallup study found that about 13 percent of the world's adults (more than 640 million people) would move permanently to another country if they could.[2] Of that number, the highest percentage of people (23 percent, or approximately 150 million) said the

United States was their destination of choice. Second on the list (with 7 percent) was the United Kingdom. The study dubbed America the undisputed "world's most desired destination for migrants." Evidently, the American dream is a big *pull*.

In Ruth's case, the biggest "push" is her mother-in-law—but Naomi's push is in the wrong direction. She isn't pushing her daughters-in-law to get out of Moab but is waging a determined campaign to send them back to Moab. Naomi isn't doing this because she is a racist but because she is a realist. Nor is she being rude. Compassionate is a more fitting description of Naomi's actions. She only means to spare them the long road of suffering ahead if they don't turn back.

Lest we romanticize life in Naomi's world, we would do well to remember that females were often bargaining chips in a male-dominated culture. Recall that Abraham and Sarah commandeered Hagar's reproductive organs to produce a son for them (Gen 16:1–5). Lot was willing to turn his daughters over to a mob of enraged sexual predators as opposed to throwing out his male guests, as the violent crowd demanded (Gen 19:4–8). Jacob's father-in-law Laban engages him in a game of chess, using his own daughters, Leah and Rachel, and two slave girls as pawns (Gen 29:16–31). Mistreatment of widows outrages YHWH and his prophets. Consider the blunt words of the prophet Isaiah. "Woe to those who ... deprive the poor of their rights and withhold justice from the oppressed of my people, *making widows their prey* and robbing the fatherless" (Isa 10:1–2, emphasis added).

In biblical times, the four most vulnerable demographics were the widow, the orphan, the poor, and the alien. And the offenses against them weren't minor. Naomi's daughters-in-law were at risk in all four categories. They were clearly widows, poor, and foreign. Given the distance between Bethlehem and Moab, even the orphan label fit them, for no father was around to defend them.

> **GOD'S HEART FOR THE FOREIGNER**
>
> "For the LORD your God is God of gods and Lord of lords, the great God, mighty and awesome, who shows no partiality and accepts no bribes. He defends the cause of the fatherless and the widow, and *loves the foreigner residing among you*, giving them food and clothing. And *you are to love those who are foreigners,* for you yourselves were foreigners in Egypt." Deuteronomy 10:17–19, emphasis added

According to Naomi's reasoning, the biggest *pull* is all about Moab. Her second attempt to get her daughters-in-law to go home is compelling. Orpah is convinced. She weeps, kisses Naomi goodbye, and heads back to Moab.

It is important to note that Orpah isn't condemned for her actions. She serves as a foil for Ruth. Her decision creates a sharp contrast with what Ruth will do, not because Orpah makes a bad choice but because her choice makes sense. Orpah's choice to return to Moab lines up with all the facts, plus she dutifully obeys her mother-in-law, as any daughter-in-law should under patriarchy. Not only that, Orpah delivers up a final clincher argument for Naomi, as the older woman launches what proved to be her last attempt to get Ruth to turn back too—Ruth, who at the moment is clinging stubbornly to her. The argument boils down to "peer pressure."

Naomi points to Orpah with approval—Orpah, whose obedient form is gradually receding on the horizon—and urges Ruth, "Look, your sister-in-law is going back to her people and her gods. Go back with her" (1:15). Naomi is commanding Ruth to leave. But this time her words transform a simple, practical decision into a theological choice. Suddenly push and pull as Naomi defines them are reversed.

Swearing on the Road to Bethlehem

Suddenly Moab owns the push and Bethlehem the pull. It is a stunning moment in the story when Naomi is outmatched by a fiercely determined daughter-in-law whose will is as immovable as granite. Through her mother-in-law's words, Ruth reaches a fork in the road where the stakes in her decision rise to the cosmic level. Now the choice is not only between Moab and Bethlehem or between Ruth's family of origin and Naomi. It is between Chemosh, Moab's god, and YHWH, the God Naomi has been railing against. Despite her mother-in-law's explicit wishes—actually Naomi's authoritative demand—and despite what onlookers might think of her, Ruth makes a radical choice. Her firm embrace of her mother-in-law turns into a determined grip. Now Ruth will tell her mother-in-law what to do.

Ruth tells Naomi to stop. As Old Testament scholar Robert L. Hubbard translates, "Do not pressure me to desert you, to give up following you" (1:16).[3] What follows is an oath unto death. Ruth swears to stick with Naomi to the grave. She will be buried with her. She then goes over Naomi's head by calling on YHWH—the God Naomi just described as her enemy—to punish her "ever so severely" if she breaks her word.

> Don't urge me to leave you or turn back from you. Where you go I will go, and where you stay I will stay. Your people will be my people and your God my God. Where you die I will die and there I will be buried. May the Lord deal with me, be it ever so severely, if even death separates you and me. (1:16–17)

Ruth employs life-threatening language—threatening her own life if she abandons Naomi. Hubbard translates the text, "*Thus* may Yahweh do to me and more so if even death itself separates me from you" (emphasis added), envisioning Ruth making a violent slashing gesture at her own throat when she says "Thus."[4]

It is impossible to imagine the impact this has on Naomi. From her point of view and according to conventional wisdom, Ruth has just thrown her life away. All we do know is that the older widow doesn't speak another word to Ruth, and that the two of them move forward together toward Bethlehem, it appears, in silence.

Ruth's passionate words have been lifted out of context and quoted in wedding ceremonies. The words themselves are exquisite and apropos for the marriage commitment. But we lose a lot when we don't take Ruth's words in context.

Her words mark a critical point in her life story, first because, as a young woman within patriarchy, making decisions wasn't part of her job description. She didn't have a voice in the matter of the husband she would marry. According to custom and culture, she didn't have a voice *in* her marriage. She would be subject to her husband's decisions, even if that involved his taking a second wife. She didn't have agency regarding her obligation to Naomi after her husband, Mahlon, died. But here, in this moment, and against the explicit will of her mother-in-law, Ruth is decisive and uses her voice. It is an earthshaking moment. She stands on her own two feet and chooses for herself. This is the first but not the last time we will see Ruth use her voice and take bold initiatives in this story.

Second, and more importantly, her decision flies in the face of the evidence Naomi put before her and that Ruth knows in her heart is the honest truth. In contrast to Orpah, Ruth rejects common sense and any shred of self-interest. The path ahead will not be easy. It will be worse for her because she will be an immigrant and her only connection is an aging widow who has no reason to live.

So what is driving Ruth? We cannot romanticize the dangerous risk she is taking or the horrible price she is almost certain to pay. Traditional interpretations offer the explanation that Ruth loves Naomi so much she cannot bear to part with her. Without a doubt, it is true Ruth loves Naomi, and, before the story is over, we will learn how woefully we've underestimated her love or how far Ruth will go in her love for Naomi. *Hesed* is major theme of the story. It is a brand of love that goes above and beyond the love humans normally offer each other. We'll dig deeper into *hesed* in the next chapter.

But loyalty or love for Naomi cannot explain what happens here. Ruth is disobeying Naomi. She is committing herself to a bleak future. And yet, she is adamant. Not only does she embrace Naomi, she embraces Naomi's people and Naomi's God.

The Turning Point

This early moment in the book of Ruth is reminiscent of the story of a confrontation between God's prophet Elijah and 450 prophets of Baal and 400 more of Asherah. Humanly speaking, it was hardly an even match. Elijah made the odds against himself even worse by dousing twelve large jars of water on the altar he wanted God to consume with fire (1 Kgs 18:16–39). Ruth's decision runs something like that. Here, while a Job story is playing out, when her mother-in-law is saying terrible things about YHWH and pushing Ruth away, and when Bethlehem promises nothing but misery and hardship, Ruth embraces Naomi and Naomi's God.

Ruth is not confused about the realities. She has watched Naomi's world collapse without a whisper of intervention from YHWH, and she herself has been swept away in the torrent of suffering. Ruth is a sufferer too. She has heard Naomi's bitter lament against YHWH. She is no fool. But when you've been living in the darkness all your life, even a flickering light has the power to *pull* you forward.

This is the power of the gospel—the choice between darkness and light. Even at her lowest point, Naomi is a light bearer. Ruth's conversion is as earthshaking and history-altering as Moses and the burning bush (Exod 3:1–10) or Saul on the road to Damascus (Acts 9:1–21). Her courageous choice to follow Naomi and YHWH into an unknown future calls to mind Abraham's response to God's call to migrate to an unknown land (Gen 12:1–3). But Ruth moves forward without hearing God's voice and without the beautiful promises that Abraham enjoyed. What will become clear, and very soon, is that the young, undocumented immigrant who arrives in Bethlehem is not the same girl as the one who left Moab. Ruth is YHWH's child now, and she will live as one.

Arrival in Bethlehem

The pair arrives in Bethlehem without further details of their journey or any conversation between them. Their arrival causes quite a stir in the village. It has been years since Elimelech, Naomi, and their two sons fled the famine in desperation. The women of Bethlehem greet Naomi. Perplexed at first, they find it hard to recognize her. Her face and posture surely reflect her pain. "Can this be Naomi?" (1:19). Surely grief and the years have taken a toll. But where are her husband and her sons? And who is this young stranger at her side?

Naomi's response reflects her demoralized state of mind. She rejects her name for a new one. Naomi means "pleasant" or "lovely." Once again she raises her voice in lament. "Call me Mara ('bitter'), because the Almighty has made my life very bitter." And then, with her daughter-in-law by her side, she adds, "I went away full, but the Lord has brought me back *empty*. Why call me Naomi? The Lord has afflicted me; the

Almighty has brought misfortune upon me" (1:20–21, emphasis added).

Her statement is an affirmation of patriarchy's value system regarding females. Naomi describes herself as "empty." Empty, with Ruth beside her, who, despite her own broken heart, has sacrificed everything to be with her and has vowed to stick with her to the very end. Naomi will always be a sufferer who to her dying day will grieve the loss of her husband and her sons. At this point in the story her grief is unbearably intense—intensified by her conviction that she has also suffered the greatest loss of all: the loss of YHWH.

Her statements stand, as they should. Who of us can criticize when we reach these kinds of lows ourselves and cannot understand why God allows bad things to happen to us? The announcement of the barley harvest signals the next chapter and the stark reminder that hunger is the first challenge they will face—the same problem that drove the family out of Bethlehem in the first place is waiting for them on their arrival.

But Naomi's suffering and her questions about YHWH suffuse the entire narrative, and we must bring them into the rest of the story with us. Has Naomi lost YHWH's love? Is he even interested in her? Is she simply doomed to run out the clock, or is God's purpose for her indestructible? And what will come from Ruth's bold decision? We must bring her radical vow with us too. The next chapter takes up Naomi's questions, but not in the way we might expect. And our undocumented friend will live up to what many Americans fear immigrants will do. Her first recorded act will be to go on Israel's welfare system.

SUGGESTED READING

- ☐ Ruth 1:14–22
- ☐ John 1:1–6

Reflection

Why did Naomi emancipate her daughters-in-law?

____

____

____

What made Ruth's choice so radical?

____

____

____

Given the combination of her own suffering and Naomi's complaint against God, what does Ruth's emphatic decision reveal about the power of the gospel?

____

____

____

How does Ruth's conversion renew hope regarding loved ones who seem hopelessly hardened to the gospel of Jesus?

____

____

____

5

THE POWER OF *HESED*

In 1956 C. S. Lewis wrote a letter to a young American writer offering the following advice: "Don't use words too big for the subject. Don't say 'infinitely' when you mean 'very'; otherwise you'll have no word left when you want to talk about something *really* infinite."[1]

Words matter, and it's easy to overstate. But there's an equally important flip side to Lewis's advice—namely, using words that are "too *small* for the subject." That "too small" problem comes up when translating the Hebrew word *hesed* into English.

Hesed is a power word in the Bible and the most important word in the book of Ruth.[2] It shows up three times, but the concept runs through the whole story and ultimately drives the action. Naomi says it first when she attempts to part from her daughters-in-law. "May the Lord show [*hesed*] to you, as you have shown to your dead and to me" (1:8). She says it again when Ruth brings home her gleanings. "He has not stopped showing his [*hesed*] to the living and the dead" (2:20). Boaz uses *hesed* to describe Ruth's actions when she proposes marriage to him. "This [*hesed*] is greater than that which you showed earlier" (3:10).

FREE LOVE!

"Two parties are involved—someone in desperate need and a second person who possesses the power and the resources to make a difference. *Hesed* is driven ... by a loyal, selfless love that motivates a person to do voluntarily what no one has a right to expect or ask of them. ... It's actually the kind of love we find most fully expressed in Jesus. In a nutshell, *hesed* is the gospel lived out." (Carolyn Custis James, *The Gospel of Ruth: Loving God Enough to Break the Rules* [Grand Rapids: Zondervan, 2008], 115)

The challenge for the reader of the book of Ruth is that English translations of *hesed* are "too small" and don't begin to convey either the power of *hesed* or its prominence in the story.

Lost in Translation

The problem with *hesed* is that English doesn't have an equivalent word for it, which puts translators in a quandary. In the search for an appropriate substitute, they offer English readers:

> A smorgasbord of words like "kindness," "mercy," "loyalty," "loving-kindness," "loyal, steadfast, unfailing (or just plain) love"—words that certainly touch on what *hesed* means but by themselves don't begin to do justice to this powerful, richly laden word. As a result, we easily skim over references

> to *hesed* without realizing we have just stumbled over one of the most potent words in the Old Testament. ... [*Hesed*] is the way God intended for human beings to live together from the beginning—the "love-your-neighbor-as-yourself" brand of living, an active, selfless, sacrificial caring for one another that goes against the grain of our fallen natures.[3]

Hesed is a costly brand of love that involves going above and beyond what anyone has a right to ask or expect. It is the brand of love at work in the actions of Ruth, Boaz, and ultimately of Naomi too.

YHWH is the ultimate *hesed*-giver. The confidence and hope of God's people banks on the fact that YHWH is "abounding in love [*hesed*]" (Exod 34:6). The weeping prophet Jeremiah comforted himself in the midst of the destruction of Jerusalem by reminding himself that "Because of the LORD's great love [*hesed*] we are not consumed, for his compassions never fail. They are new every morning; great is your faithfulness" (Lam 3:21–23).

The book of Ruth puts God's *hesed* on display. We will learn along with Naomi that God's *hesed* love is indiscriminate, unearned, and persistent. YHWH's *hesed* will reach Naomi through the selfless and relentless commitment of Ruth to fight for her, and Boaz will join Ruth in this effort. Events in the field of Boaz this day will give Naomi fresh insight into YHWH's *hesed*. What she learns is indispensible to us—because so often we struggle to put suffering and God's *hesed* together in our own stories.

Battling Hunger

Apparently the morning after arriving in Bethlehem, Naomi is engulfed in grief and hopelessness. She's convinced YHWH's *hesed* for her has evaporated, and he has turned against her. From Naomi's perspective, it appears that YHWH has destroyed her past and stolen her future. She has given up on life. So it is not surprising that she takes a rather passive role in tackling the first challenge they face on their arrival in Bethlehem. They have no food.

Not so Ruth, who initiates the action, despite her own grief and the insecurities that naturally accompany arrival in a foreign country. She has not forgotten her impassioned vow to care for her mother-in-law. She wastes no time making good on her promise. She decides to glean, and Naomi gives her consent. "Go ahead my daughter" (2:2).

Gleaning was Israel's welfare system—a way for the poor, the widow, the orphan, and the alien to sustain themselves by scavenging leftover grain from community fields. The Mosaic gleaning law (Lev 19:9–10; Deut 24:19–22) required a landowner to leave the corners and edges of his field unharvested. After clearing the field, harvesters were not allowed to go back for grain they missed but were to "leave what remains for the foreigner, the fatherless and the widow" (Deut 24:20).

Hired male harvesters cut the grain, and female harvesters followed to gather the grain into bundles to be carted off to the threshing floor. Once the harvesters were finished, gleaners could gather up whatever scraps remained.

In an ancient Near Eastern shame-based culture, gleaning was a source of shame. It was a public display of poverty. In Israel, "poverty itself was not a moral problem. The problems for Israelites were the loss of status and shame that poverty entailed."[4] As Hubbard explains, "The gleaning of fallen grain was mere subsistence living, much like trying to eke out survival today by recycling aluminum cans."[5] In Israel, for someone like Naomi, who was once a respected member of the Bethlehem community, it must have been a blow to her sense of dignity for her daughter-in-law to join the ranks of gleaners. Scholar André LaCocque notes, "The brevity of the permission given to Ruth here (2:2) expresses [Naomi's] despondency: the two women had arrived at the bitter end—at subsistence. They have nothing more to lose."[6]

Danger in the Promised Land

We do Ruth an enormous disservice if we fail to acknowledge the risks involved in her decision to become a gleaner. This was the dreaded day when Ruth would come face-to-face with the reasons Naomi warned her to go home. Ruth's decision to venture out alone into a foreign culture without a friend in the world was precarious, to say the least. The prospect of harm surely compounded Naomi's fragile state of mind by adding a boatload of anxiety that day.

We must not minimize the serious threats unprotected women have historically faced—a reality for Ruth that both Naomi and Boaz underscore. To protect Ruth from abuse or injury in his field, Boaz instructs his male harvesters "not to lay a hand on" her (2:9). At the end of the day, when Ruth returns home safely, a relieved Naomi urges her to continue gleaning in this particular field "because in someone else's field you might be harmed" (2:22).

RUTH'S AUDACIOUS REQUEST

If Ruth is asking Boaz for permission to glean, she is drawing unnecessary and potentially dangerous attention to herself by asking for permission to do what the Mosaic law required and Boaz already allowed. According to more recent scholarship, Ruth "has evidently elected to request permission to go beyond normal custom. … Given the meager fare gleaners probably gathered, one suspects a concern to increase her chances of gleaning enough to provide for Naomi and herself. In any case, Ruth showed herself to be anything but a modest, self-effacing foreigner. Rather, she emerges as courageous if not slightly brash. … She willingly took a sizable risk in order to benefit her mother-in-law". (Robert J. Hubbard Jr., *The Book of Ruth*, New International Commentary on the Old Testament [Grand Rapids: Eerdmans, 1988], 149–50)

Danger threatens Ruth from three different fronts. First, she faces danger from other hungry gleaners who were scrambling for scant gleanings. The presence of one more gleaner obviously means less for everyone else. The barley field could easily become a battlefield as gleaners competed and fought over limited resources. Young, female, foreign, and presumably wearing garments that marked her out as a widow, Ruth is an easy target for greedy gleaners who might choose to seize whatever grain she managed to collect.

Second, she faces danger at the hands of the hired harvesters. Before Boaz even speaks to her, he has drawn a line around her that his workers must not cross and might have otherwise. Harvesters were common laborers who worked under the thumb of the landowner. Their daily take-home pay—a half-pound to a pound of grain, according to ancient Babylonian records[7]—would never get them ahead.

Harvesters occupied a low level in Bethlehem's power pyramid, but gleaners ranked even lower. Harvesters could find it tempting to take out their resentments on gleaners by pulling rank and mistreating them. The tendency among humans to pass their pain and frustrations onto those less powerful and less fortunate is a recurring blight on human history. It happens at every level of patriarchal cultural structures. So for a young, defenseless woman like Ruth, the possibility of sexual assault is present ... even in the field of Boaz.

Third and most surprising, Boaz also poses a threat. The storyteller opens this scene by introducing Boaz as a towering figure. *Hayil* is the Hebrew word the narrator uses to describe Boaz. It indicates he is a man of valor, stature, wealth, privilege, and power. The word *hayil* conjures up images of an "elite warrior similar to the hero of the Homeric epic."[8] Considering that "the days when the judges ruled" were characterized by frequent wars, Boaz may have been a military hero. He is also identified twice as Elimelech's relative, a fact Naomi later confirms (2:1, 3b, 20).

Ruth is not privy to any of this information. From her perspective, Boaz simply represents power. The disparity between the two of them couldn't be more pronounced, and we are supposed to notice. The story is intended to pose the question: What will Boaz do with his power? From Ruth's perspective, Boaz is a serious threat. The world is full of stories of powerful village strongmen who abuse their powers especially against widows in horrific ways. So it is astonishing that before Boaz even arrives, and without knowing whether he is safe, Ruth has already taken a gutsy chance.

Sanctuary

That Ruth ends up in the field of Boaz is not mere happenstance. Clearly YHWH is providentially guiding the steps of his daughter to this particular field. But we minimize YWHW's place in the story if we fail to recognize how powerfully he is working in other ways and, in particular, on Naomi's behalf. Ruth's arrival in the field of Boaz marks the beginning of a divine shake-up in the village of Bethlehem.

Traditional interpretations view Boaz as the true leader and hero of the story, assuming this powerful, rich, man of valor will reverse the flagging fortunes of the two widows. But it is Ruth who proves to be the true leader in the story as she seeks to live as YHWH's child and battles on Naomi's behalf. Her actions demonstrate a vibrant, radical faith to a community that has settled for precision obedience to God's law.

By the time Boaz arrives on the scene, YHWH is already powerfully present in his field through the young Moabite immigrant who will dare to challenge the system and upend the status quo. When Ruth arrives at the barley field of Boaz, she is in battle mode for Naomi. Even before Boaz speaks in her defense, she has found sanctuary—not in culturally recognized safe zones or under the protection of a man. She has found refuge under YHWH's wing, and that is the solid base from which she operates.

The Hungry Side of the Law

Boaz sees a newcomer in his field and learns from his overseer that "she is the Moabite who came back from Moab with Naomi" (2:6). The overseer then proceeds to tell his boss about Ruth's audacious request.

It goes without saying that gleaning wasn't a lucrative business. This hand-to-mouth existence is still practiced in today's world. Locally, it often amounts to rummaging through a garbage bin outside McDonald's in search of someone's leftover Big Mac or a few discarded fries. The odds are slim that Ruth will return home with enough for Naomi and herself, especially with other gleaners competing for whatever grain remains.

Boaz is an honorable man who complies with Mosaic law. He permits gleaners in his field. But Ruth doesn't want to take home scraps to her mother-in-law. So she makes a bold, even outrageous proposal to Boaz. Instead of scavenging for snippets of grain, she wants to glean where freshly cut grain is lying on the ground.

Ruth lives on the hungry side of the law, and the law looks very different from that point of view. Her proposal presses Boaz beyond the letter of the law to fulfill its spirit. The letter of the law says, "Let them glean." The spirit of the law says, "Feed them."

Her brazen request creates a healthy conflict of interest for Boaz, as it should. The gleaning law doesn't specify how wide is an edge or how big is a corner or how scrupulously harvesters are to clear the field. Undoubtedly landowners always wrestled with how much to leave for those with less and how much to keep for themselves, but in the aftermath of a prolonged and devastating famine, the struggle would be especially difficult.

Instead of taking offense, Boaz's response is as radical as Ruth's proposal. This powerhouse of a man, this native-born Israelite who grew up on Mosaic law, listens to this newcomer's request, learns from her, and throws his power behind her effort. He is obviously committed to God's law, but his actions here and later at the threshing floor demonstrate "his willingness to adopt a broader interpretation of it."[9] He, like others in Bethlehem, is in awe of what she has done for Naomi.

He swiftly issues a series of executive orders to guarantee her success. Not only does he ensure her safety, as she, with his permission, ventures into territory that is normally off-limits to gleaners, but he fuels her efforts by providing food and water. At mealtime he invites her to join his workers and serves her a meal of roasted grain, giving her more than she can eat. He grants her access to water drawn by his male workers. He further instructs his harvesters to pull out stalks of grain from the bundles and place them in her path so she can glean even more. In the end she will take home far more than any of his harvesters will earn in a day of labor.

Naomi Revives

Naomi's astonishment upon Ruth's return is one of the priceless whiplash moments in the Bible. After what must have been a miserable day of anxiety for her, Naomi's worst fears aren't realized. Ruth doesn't arrive shattered with accounts of violence and rape. Instead, she walks in the door with twenty-nine pounds of winnowed barley—at least half a month's pay for a male harvester. Then she presents her hungry mother-in-law the leftover roasted grain from the meal Boaz served her. It's the first fast-food meal in the Bible.

It is hard to describe Naomi's surprise as her excited questions and words of blessing spill out. "Where did you glean today? Where did you work? Blessed be the man who took notice of you!"(2:19) It is obvious to Naomi that it was impossible for Ruth to glean so much without extraordinary help.

When she learns the man is Boaz, her exuberance continues. "The LORD bless him! ... He has not stopped showing his kindness [*hesed*] to the living and the dead" (2:20). In the Hebrew text, the "he" is ambiguous in "*He* has not stopped showing his kindness [*hesed*] to the living and the dead." Is she referring to Boaz or YHWH? The ambiguity invites the answer "Both!" YHWH's preferred method of getting things done is to work through his image bearers. So YHWH's *hesed* comes to Naomi through her daughter-in-law and now also through Boaz.

It is a dramatic turning point for this female Job. This is the moment when Naomi's hope in YHWH revives—not because she senses a budding romance, nor because a little good fortune cures her heartache. It is a turning point for her because she senses YHWH's *hesed* in the unexpected abundance of barley before her.

Grief sensitizes God's child to any evidence of God's presence. In the dark, we strain our eyes for the slightest sign of him. Something Naomi would never have noticed in more prosperous times speaks volumes of *hesed* to her YHWH-starved soul and, in essence, raises Naomi from the dead.

Awareness of God's unfailing *hesed* for her breathes new life into grieving Naomi's soul. YHWH loves her after all. Although she is a zero in the eyes of the culture, although she has lost everything that might cause him to value her, although her life has been reduced to rubble, and her future is destroyed, YHWH is not finished with Naomi yet. YHWH has strategic kingdom work for Naomi that she will be uniquely equipped to do.

The Naomi we encounter hereafter isn't thinking of herself. She is focused on her daughter-in-law Ruth and so becomes a *hesed* giver too. And Ruth in the following scene will put good use to the information she picks up here from Naomi. "The man is our close relative; he is one of our kinsman redeemers" (2:20).

SUGGESTED READING

- ☐ Ruth 2:1–23
- ☐ Psalm 13:5

Reflection

What is *hesed*, and how does it exceed the words used for it in English translations (e.g., "kindness," "loving kindness," "mercy," "love," "unfailing love")?

___

___

___

How do Ruth, Boaz, and the harvesters display *hesed* in the barley field?

Why was Naomi convinced she had lost God's *hesed*, and what convinced her she was wrong?

Describe a situation in your own life that spoke God's *hesed* for you.

6

*REST*LESS IN BETHLEHEM

Certain episodes in the Bible make us uneasy, especially when anything of a sexual nature is involved. Either we ignore the subject altogether and focus on another aspect of the story, or we interpret it gingerly in ways that, more often than not, paint a negative picture of the woman involved.

Matthew's genealogy of Jesus breaks with normal practice by including four women in what is normally an all-male list. All four women who made the list are best remembered for stories that are especially notorious for sexual content. Tamar the Canaanite, Judah's twice-widowed daughter-in-law, poses as a prostitute and becomes pregnant by her father in-law, Judah. Rahab is the Canaanite prostitute who, along with her family, is spared during Israel's attack on Jericho. Moderns have accused Ruth the Moabitess of seducing Boaz in their notorious threshing-floor encounter. Then there's Bathsheba, who allegedly enticed King David into committing adultery.

It seems to go unnoticed (or perhaps may be hard to swallow) that Scripture vindicates all four women.

Judah condemns himself and exonerates Tamar when he says, "She is righteous, I am not,"[1] and Tamar is referenced with honor in a wedding blessing for Boaz and Ruth (Ruth 4:12). Rahab makes the Hebrews 11 list of people for her courageous, life-risking faith in harboring Israelite spies (Heb 11:31). When the prophet Nathan confronts King David over his sin against Uriah the Hittite and Bathsheba, he doesn't condemn Bathsheba or label her as a seductress. He calls her "a lamb" (2 Sam 12:1–6)—not an accomplice but a victim of David's actions, which many believe were rape.[2]

The tendency to suspect women of seduction and treachery has long roots that go back to the garden of Eden and is reinforced by centuries of church teaching. The words of revered medieval church father Albert the Great have had an unfortunate sticking power.

> Woman is a misbegotten man and has a faulty and defective nature. ... What she cannot get, she seeks to obtain through lying and diabolical deceptions. And so, to put it briefly, one must be on one's guard with every woman, as if she were a poisonous snake and a horned devil. ... Thus in evil and perverse doings woman is cleverer, that is, slyer, than man. Her feelings drive woman toward every evil, just as reason impels man toward all good.[3]

Although Ruth remains one of the most admired women in all of Scripture, even she comes under scrutiny for her conduct at the threshing floor. What is she doing when she uncovers Boaz's feet?

Naomi's Strategy

Most noticeable in this mysterious episode is the dramatic change we observe in Naomi. We are mistaken to imagine she has gotten over her losses. Sorrow will accompany Naomi to her grave. That is the price of love, as those who have lost a loved one know all too well.

The change in Naomi results from her rediscovery of YHWH'S *hesed*. That frees her from being self-absorbed in grief to focus now on Ruth. In a real sense, Naomi's initial concerns for Ruth have never changed. Ruth's situation is every bit as desperate and her future as every bit as bleak as Naomi described on the road to Bethlehem. Only now there is the added prospect of Ruth outliving Naomi and ending up stranded in a foreign country. Naomi fears for Ruth's future and intends to do something about it.

It is unfair to Naomi to suggest she is playing matchmaker in the usual way or that she has hopes of a potential pregnancy and a baby in mind. Having suffered through ten years of barrenness with her daughter-in-law, it would be the height of cruelty to reopen that painful chapter. It is also invalid to imagine she is worried about how they will survive the coming winter now that the harvest season is over. Ruth's ongoing gleaning supported by Boaz's advocacy ensures they will have plenty.

Two words reveal Naomi's purpose. The first is "rest"— the same objective she had in mind when she pressed her daughters-in-law to go back to Moab. "May the Lord grant that each of you will find *rest* in the home of another husband" (1:9). Now she brings it up again, saying to Ruth, "My daughter, I must find [*rest*] for you, where you will be well provided for" (3:1).

The second word is how she identifies Boaz, *not* with legal language as their kinsman-redeemer (*go'el*), but as a "relative." The former comes with legal responsibilities. The latter is simply a reason to hope family relations will incline him to be receptive to her plan.

Even so, her mission faces what many would regard as insurmountable odds. Ruth is foreign, poor, and barren. She brings nothing of advantage to a marriage—no social connections, no wealth, and no prospect of offspring. It is irrational to think any respectable man would choose a barren woman for a bride. Given the lack of a male go-between to negotiate a marriage, Naomi must resort to irregular and decidedly risky methods.

Before the clock runs out for Naomi, she will take extraordinary measures to see her daughter-in-law safely situated under the protective umbrella of a husband. Naomi isn't looking to give Boaz the girl he has been too hesitant to pursue. Naomi is looking for mercy.

Naomi's scheme is fraught with risk. She sends Ruth out alone in the night, bathed, perfumed, and wearing her best clothes, not her widow's garb, to signal her readiness for marriage. The risks are heightened because now that harvest is over villagers are celebrating—eating and drinking at the threshing floor. Not to be naïve about the dangers, it is important to note that threshing-floor celebrations had a reputation for drunkenness and immorality.[4]

No parent in their right mind would send their daughter out alone into the night under circumstances like that. Naomi is banking on what she knows of Boaz that he won't take sexual advantage of Ruth. Under cover of darkness, he is free to refuse without publicly humiliating Ruth.

The threshing floor was an open space outside the village proper where bundles of grain were carried for winnowing and where harvesters could count on a strong breeze. Harvesters would spread stalks of grain on the ground, where animal hooves, a weighted threshing sledge dragged by oxen, or workers beating grain with sticks separated the grain from the husks. Then harvesters would toss the mixture into the air with a shovel, and the breeze would blow the chaff away, while the heavier kernels of grain would fall to the ground.

Naomi instructs Ruth to remain hidden until Boaz finishes eating and drinking and is in good spirits. She must watch carefully to see where he retires for the night. It would be disastrous to approach the wrong man. When he is sleeping, she is to go to him, uncover his feet, and wait for him to tell her what to do.[5]

Ruth responds, "I will do whatever you say."

Shock and Awe

The evening finds Boaz a happy man. After years of famine, he has enjoyed a successful harvest and has reached out generously—gone above and beyond the gleaning law—to aid the poor. Tonight he will sleep a contented man, albeit with one eye open, guarding what belongs to him.

Ruth scrupulously follows Naomi's instructions. She watches and waits in the darkness. When all is quiet—except for the occasional snore—she makes her way stealthily to where the unsuspecting Boaz is sleeping peacefully. As Naomi instructed, Ruth uncovers his feet, lies down, and waits some more.

The situation is actually comical. This highly esteemed man of valor, this conscientious, buttoned-down Israelite who is in impeccable compliance with Mosaic law, this happy man sleeping contentedly under the stars after a successful harvest, feels the cool night air on his feet. He awakens to the shock of a woman in the darkness lying at his feet.

It would be worth a lot to have seen his face! Or to have heard his raspy, suddenly wide-awake question, "Who are you?"

Her response is straightforward enough: "I am your servant Ruth." If he was shocked to find a woman at his feet, no words can describe his astonishment—his awe—at what she says next. Instead of waiting as Naomi instructed for Boaz to tell her "what to do," Ruth tosses Naomi's script to follow her own. She instructs Boaz. "Spread the corner of your garment over me, since you are a kinsman-redeemer [*go'el*]" (3:9).

Although it may suit Western notions of romance to portray Boaz as an eligible older bachelor, within patriarchy a man who postpones marriage and delays fathering sons to secure his family's survival for another generation would never be regarded as *hayil*. To the contrary, he would be an unworthy son, a disgrace, a shame to his family.

As we learned from Naomi's story, a family without sons faces a crisis of dramatic proportions. In today's Middle East, a Palestinian husband who was actually in that predicament when his wife failed to produce any sons lamented desperately, "I am *nothing* in this village without a son!"[6] Boaz is a man of significant stature in the Bethlehem community. Boaz had sons. We don't know whether he was a widower or had a living wife (or two). The narrator doesn't tell us. But bachelors are a modern phenomenon, and Boaz wasn't one.

The Real Rescue

Without a doubt, the most surprising twist in the story is that Ruth isn't being rescued as Naomi intended.[7] Ruth is the one launching a rescue, and the person she intends to rescue is her deceased father-in-law, Elimelech, whose legacy is dying out. She initiates that rescue when her proposal to Boaz turns legal, and she confronts him with two Mosaic laws concerned with rescuing men.

The *kinsman-redeemer law* requires the nearest relative to purchase a man's land if he is forced to sell.[8] The *levirate law* requires the blood brother of a man who dies without a male heir to marry his widow.[9] The first son born to their union takes the place of the dead man on the family tree, including his inheritance (Deut 25:5–9).

Ruth's proposal again moves the discussion of the law from the *letter* to the *spirit*, as Jesus does generations later in his Sermon on the Mount. Boaz is neither the nearest relative nor Elimelech's blood brother. He is beyond the reach of the letter of the law, but not its spirit.

The reality is that Ruth isn't seeking a husband for herself. Still committed to her vow, she is battling for Naomi, and in an act of unparalleled faith, barren Ruth volunteers to bear a son. Boaz understands what she is doing for Naomi's family, and he is awestruck. He blesses and praises her for her *hesed* for Naomi and calls her a woman of valor [*hayil*] (3:11). It is a moment to ponder. Boaz is rejecting the culture's value system regarding women by valuing Ruth not for her beauty, her male connections, or her ability to produce a son, but for her character and for her radical, sacrificial love for Naomi.

WHO TAKES CHARGE AT THE THRESHING FLOOR?

"Boaz, says Naomi, will tell Ruth what to do; Ruth will do what her mother-in-law tells her; Boaz 'surrenders his weapons' and will adjust himself to Ruth's decision. In short, Ruth is now the central agent of the events. The older generation relies on the younger, the one of higher social status on the lower, the stronger of the world on the weaker (1 Cor 1:27), masculine authority on female wisdom. In Ruth 2:1 Boaz was a 'man of substance' [*hayil*]; now he recognizes in Ruth a 'woman of substance' [*hayil*] (3:11). Such a reversal of values is at the very least subversive." (André LaCocque, *Ruth*, trans. K. C. Hanson [Minneapolis: Fortress, 2004], 92)

That said, her appeal to the law changes everything. Instead of a simple marriage arrangement, as Naomi hoped, Boaz reveals the existence of a nearer kinsman-redeemer who has first rights to Elimelech's land and whose rights must be honored.[10] Still, Boaz vows that if the nearer kinsman refuses, he will fulfill her request (3:10–13).

It is too late for Ruth to return to Bethlehem without giving the impression that something untoward has happened. So Boaz instructs her to remain until morning, when he sends her back to Naomi with a *seah* (sixty to a hundred pounds) of grain as a sign of his intention to settle the matter for her family. True to his word, Boaz heads for Bethlehem straightaway. And Naomi, completely gobsmacked for the second time, assures Ruth, "The man will not *rest* until the matter is settled today" (3:18, emphasis added).

SUGGESTED READING

- ☐ Ruth 3:1–18
- ☐ Philippians 2:1–8

Reflection

What did Naomi hope to accomplish by sending Ruth to Boaz at the threshing floor—a potentially dangerous situation?

____

____

____

How does Naomi's description of Boaz as a "relative" versus Ruth's addressing him as *go'el* (kinsman-redeemer) reveal that the two women have different objectives? How are they sacrificing for each other?

____

____

____

Why did Boaz characterize and praise Ruth's actions as *hesed* ("kindness" in 3:10)?

How can *hesed* make a difference in our own choices and actions on behalf of others?

7

BREAKING THE RULES FOR NAOMI

General Douglas MacArthur (1880–1964) is credited with saying, "You are remembered for the rules you break, not the rules you follow." That statement seems ironic coming from someone in the military, where the chain of command prevails and soldiers strictly follow orders. In MacArthur's case, breaking the rules came with mixed results. It led to his rise as a highly decorated military leader, to his success as commander in the Pacific Theater of WWII, and his leadership in the reconstruction of postwar Japan. It also led to his downfall when the rules he broke risked war with China and affected his relationship with President Truman, who ultimately relieved MacArthur of his duties.

Sometimes breaking the rules can backfire. But breaking the rules can also be a good thing and often leads to progress. In fact, progress won't happen if people always insist on coloring inside the lines instead of imagining something bold and new. Innovation and creativity often require thinking and acting outside the box. As the saying goes, "Some rules were made to be broken."

When Mosaic laws get broken in Bethlehem, a whole new realm of possibilities opens up for what it means to live as God's child, revealing a radical way of being human in relationships with others. The gospel is, by its very nature, countercultural.

The natural human inclination is to be minimalist when it comes to obeying Scripture. That's what Boaz was doing when he "allowed" gleaners in his field. His compliance with the law may well have contributed to his reputation as *hayil*. But precise obedience to the letter of the gleaning law could easily send weary gleaners home after a long day toiling in the hot sun with too little to feed their families. Ruth's request broke open the gleaning law to reveal the unbounded nature of God's love.

When Naomi sent her daughter-in-law out into the night, she had no idea that Ruth would be breaking the law again—turning a private request for marriage into a public legal matter. One wonders whether she would have sent Ruth to the threshing floor in the first place if she had known her daughter-in-law's actions would end up involving all Bethlehem or that ultimately city elders would be witnessing her daughter-in-law's revolutionary reinterpretation of God's law.

Ruth was no General MacArthur. She didn't speak from a position of power or authority. To the contrary, she approached Boaz as a petitioner coming from the margins, a powerless outsider, "the other." Yet, she deserves to be remembered (and emulated) for the rules she broke—three in all—and all of them on behalf of Naomi. First, Ruth pressed the boundaries of the gleaning law. Then she broke two more laws in her proposal to Boaz. She not only breaks open both the levirate and kinsman-redeemer laws, but she fuses them to exceed what Naomi intended to be a simple appeal for marriage.

Break It Like Ruth!

En route from Moab to Bethlehem, Naomi made it clear that her losses were irrevocable. Israelite laws designed to provide assistance to a family in crisis no longer applied to her, first because there were no surviving males in her family, and second because Naomi's childbearing years had expired.

The kinsman-redeemer law went into effect when a man became poor and was compelled to sell his land. According to the law, his nearest male relative was responsible to buy his land to ensure that tribal land remained within the tribe. The price of the property was based on the number of harvests until the Year of Jubilee, when the property would revert back to the original owner (Lev 25:25–28). But there is no man alive to sell Elimelech's land.

Now that the famine is over, it appears that Elimelech's *go'els* (kinsman-redeemers) are preoccupied with famine recovery and focused on their own land. Meanwhile, Elimelech's land lies fallow. It would be addressed at a future date when, most likely, the nearest relative would inherit Elimelech's property simply by default, since neither Naomi nor Ruth has sons.

The levirate law is the first Mosaic law mentioned in the book of Ruth. Naomi referred to it in despair on the road from Moab when she said, "Am I going to have any more sons who could become your husbands? ... I am too old to have another husband. Even if I thought there was still hope for me—even if I had a husband tonight and then gave birth to sons—would you wait until they grew up? Would you remain unmarried for them?" (1:11–13).

The levirate law centered on progeny and was *unrelated* to kinsman-redeemer responsibilities. It involved producing a male heir for a deceased brother. The family line stopped with Elimelech. The narrator doesn't identify any man in the story as Elimelech's brother, and besides, what does it matter, since Naomi is too old to conceive a child? The levirate law is irrelevant to her family, or so she thinks.

It takes an outsider like Ruth to figure out a way around this impasse by combining the two laws and expanding their reach. Real estate and progeny (not romance) were on her mind when she proposed marriage to Boaz. Her intentions were perfectly clear to him when she joined her request for marriage ("Spread the corner of your garment over me") with a reference to family obligations for Elimelech's land ("for you are a *go'el* of our family"). In a single, innovative sentence Ruth merged the levirate and kinsman-redeemer laws—property and progeny. She was asking Boaz to purchase Elimelech's land and to father a son to become Elimelech's heir and the eventual owner of his land.

Ruth was taking an enormous risk when she confronted Boaz with family responsibility at the threshing floor and challenged him to help her rescue Naomi's family. Given the traditional understanding of those laws, what chance was there that anyone would agree to such a plan?

Turns out, Boaz was as much of a rule breaker as Ruth.

Boaz Goes to Town

Boaz takes the lead in this part of the story. Naomi was right to say that he wouldn't rest until he settled the matter. He heads straight for the Bethlehem city gate,[1] where he will assemble a quorum of elders to witness him presenting Ruth's proposal to Elimelech's nearest *go'el*.[2] Although no one knew it at the time, these events at the city gate would become one of the greatest moments in the history of Bethlehem.

> **THE CITY GATE**
>
> "In ancient times, the city gate was not only the point of entry into town and the most logical place to look for fellow villagers coming and going, it was also the heart of the community. The gate was the seat of government and the site of important business transactions, a platform for local dignitaries, a pulpit for prophetic messages, and the hub of local gossip for the entire village. So whenever you hear of someone being praised in the gates (like the legendary woman of Proverbs 31), the entire community from the top down is honoring them." (Carolyn Custis James, *The Gospel of Ruth: Loving God Enough to Break the Rules* [Grand Rapids: Zondervan, 2008], 178)

As if on queue, the nearer kinsman-redeemer appears right away. Boaz pulls him aside, gathers ten elders, and proceeds to make a case for Naomi, who, he announces, is selling Elimelech's land. Boaz, like an attorney worth every cent his client pays, proceeds with a shrewdly crafted strategy that proves both powerful and effective.

The Old Testament doesn't contain any provision for a widow to inherit her husband's land. In ancient Israel, property rights focused on men. The only exception resulted when Zelophehad only fathered daughters. Moses granted his daughters the right to inherit their father's land so long as they married men within their tribe. But individual women didn't inherit land. Yet here, in a surprising move, Boaz proves to be Ruth's partner in crime, for he bends the law to invest Naomi with property rights, as well as the right to sell Elimelech's land (Num 36:1–12). At the same time Boaz fast-tracks the issue of her land by presenting the nearest kinsman with first rights to purchase the land now, noting that if the nearer *go'el* refuses, he (Boaz) is next in line and ready to buy.

From every angle, Boaz is offering a lucrative investment. Regardless of what it costs up front, the lack of an Elimelech heir means the nearer kinsman will double his property holdings and his own sons will inherit more.

The nearer kinsman-redeemer knows a good deal when he sees it. So he responds, "I will redeem it" (4:4).

The Big Gamble

That's when Boaz adds one more condition that turns the entire transaction on its head. "On the day you buy the land from Naomi, you also acquire Ruth the Moabite, *the dead man's widow*, in order to maintain the name of the dead with his property" (4:5, emphasis added).

Suddenly, the original lucrative investment becomes a high-stakes gamble. If the nearer kinsman-redeemer marries Ruth, and she remains barren, he will inherit everything. But if she conceives a son, her son will inherit Elimelech's land. Everything the nearer kinsman invests will go to Ruth's son, and his own sons will inherit less.

On the one hand, after ten years of marriage to Mahlon, Ruth's barrenness is hardly a secret. And yet... on the other hand, if Ruth gives birth to a son, it will "endanger [his] own estate" (4:6). It's a potentially ruinous gamble he can't afford to take. To Boaz he says, "You redeem it yourself. I cannot do it" (4:6).[3]

It's easy to overlook the profound impact of this story in the jubilant hubbub that follows—the subsequent marriage of Boaz and Ruth and the celebratory words of the elders and the people at the city gate. Deeper things are going on that get lost if we think this story offers a picture-perfect ending, complete with a wedding, a baby, a contented Naomi, and a "happily-ever-after" banner waving over the end.

O Little Town of Bethlehem

According to history, the little town of Bethlehem was always destined for greatness. Small in comparison to other cities, it secured a dominant place in Jewish history as the birthplace of Israel's King David and the location of Samuel's priestly anointing of the young shepherd boy as Israel's second king.

But even that wasn't Bethlehem's most significant reason for greatness. The prophet Micah spoke of an even greater day for Bethlehem. "But you, Bethlehem Ephrathah, though you are small among the clans of Judah, out of you will come for me one who will be ruler over Israel, whose origins are from of old, from ancient times" (Mic 5:2). Generations later, the birth of Jesus the Messiah forever distinguished Bethlehem from every other city or town on the planet. Every Christmas, year after year, thousands of Christians make a pilgrimage to Bethlehem in honor of the birth of Jesus, who forever secured that little town's greatness.

But the legacy of Bethlehem's greatness can be traced back earlier than King David to the dark, tumultuous era "when the judges ruled." It all began when a Moabite immigrant crossed the border into Israel and made a fierce commitment to live as YHWH's child. She brought a fresh perspective to Mosaic law. She refused to settle for mere obedience to the letter of the law when its vast spiritual possibilities lay before her.

Hesed transforms legality into sacrificial love, gives life amid despair, and draws one deeper into the heart of YHWH. The collaboration between Ruth and Boaz breathes new hope and life into a devastated Naomi, who despite her grief and losses turns outward to care about Ruth's future. She comes up with a strategy to spare her daughter-in-law from endless isolation and suffering in Bethlehem's margins. Naomi is giving Ruth up, when Ruth is all she has. This is the widow's mite.

Ruth reopens a painful chapter of her life and risks public humiliation if she fails to bear a son. But she is relentless in turning every situation back to Naomi's benefit. This is the life that *hesed* produces.

Boaz will purchase Naomi's land and marry Ruth, who will give birth to a son. The fears of Elimelech's nearer kinsman will fall on Boaz, who is willing to risk financial ruin and ultimately pays that price to father a son for Elimelech. But the gospel reminds us all that we are our brother's keeper.

Bethlehem's greatness can be traced to the healthy kind of rule breaking that results when God's people use their imaginations to pursue the spirit of the law. Together Naomi, Ruth, and Boaz make sacrifices that foreshadow the gospel of Jesus.

SUGGESTED READING

- ☐ Ruth 4:1–12
- ☐ Matthew 5:17–48; 22:36–40

Reflection

How does Boaz advocate for Naomi in Bethlehem's court of law?

___

___

___

How is the spirit versus the letter of Mosaic law put into effect?

___

___

___

How do the actions of Ruth and Boaz on Naomi's behalf foreshadow what Jesus is teaching in his Sermon on the Mount in Matthew 5?

____

____

____

How does this kind of rule breaking help you imagine the endless possibilities to the greatest commandments: "Love the Lord your God with all your heart and with all your soul and with all your mind" and "Love your neighbor as yourself"?

____

____

____

8

THE MANLY SIDE OF THE STORY

In 2013, esteemed newsman Tom Brokaw predicted that the twenty-first century will be known as "the Century of Women."[1] In her grimly titled book *The End of Men—and the Rise of Women*, journalist Hanna Rosin confirms his thesis and examines the flip side of this development. Her research (which is surprisingly sympathetic to men) substantiates that current social, cultural, and economic changes are benefiting women and disadvantaging a lot of men. "For nearly as long as civilization has existed, patriarchy ... has been the organizing principle, with few exceptions."[2]

Now all that is changing.

Traditional roles are becoming more fluid, and definitions of what it means to be "a real man" are not as clear or attainable as in the past. A man's previously secure status as the chief decider, breadwinner, and protector is eroding.

Men must compete with women for jobs. Jobs are disappearing as computers replace men and whole industries shut down or move overseas. Furthermore, a lot of men are working in jobs where their boss is a woman. As one man lamented,

> Women live longer than men. They do better in this economy. More of 'em graduate from college. They go into space and do everything men do, and sometimes they do it a whole lot better. I mean, hell, get out of the way—these females are going to leave us males in the dust.[3]

It seems the pendulum that favored men for millennia has swung in favor of women.

The Swinging Pendulum

Anyone reading the book of Ruth might suspect that even here the pendulum is swinging in favor of women. The first few lines of the story seem to bolster that theory.

Elimelech is the first person mentioned in the story (1:1). In keeping with typical patriarchal protocol, all three members of his family are identified in relation to him: "*His* wife's name was Naomi and the names of *his* two sons were Mahlon and Kilion" (1:2, emphasis added).

Yet instead of a story featuring Elimelech and his sons, calamity strikes, and in five brief verses all three men die and are buried in Moab—far removed, it seems, from the main action of the story. Remarkably, the narrator doesn't abort the story, now that it is devoid of men. Instead the spotlight shifts seamlessly to their three surviving widows, and the story continues.

From this point on, the story belongs to Naomi. One commentator underscores the atypical nature of this shift, especially within the ancient patriarchal context. "Interestingly [Elimelech] is called *Naomi's husband*, though it is rare for a man to be characterized with reference to a woman" (emphasis original). That commentator finishes off Elimelech by adding, "In this story [Elimelech] *plays no part*" (emphasis added).[4]

The rest of the story pivots on decisions women are making. In fact, Ruth drives the action, not merely in her decision to go with Naomi to Bethlehem or to glean but by venturing into sacred territory at the heart of the Jewish culture when she reinterprets Mosaic law. And in a shocking role reversal, Boaz responds to her initiatives.

Given how the story turns things upside down, it's easy to believe the pendulum in this story is swinging in favor of women and at the expense of men. But nothing could be further from the truth. Despite evidence to the contrary, *from start to finish the book of Ruth is all about men*. Much deeper matters are afoot than another round in the battle of the sexes.

It's a big mistake to conclude that "in this story [Elimelech] plays no part." Elimelech and his sons show up in every chapter. Their interests are paramount to everything that happens. Furthermore, the story puts on display a brand of masculinity that is desperately needed in a world awash in changes today that strike at the core of masculine identity and leave so many men adrift without a sense of meaning or purpose. The book of Ruth has plenty to say about and to men that goes much deeper than a cultural pendulum swing. To be sure, it conveys a powerful message for women and girls that doesn't come at the expense of men. But the book of Ruth simultaneously puts on display a radical, not-of-this-world brand of masculinity that foreshadows the masculinity Jesus embodied.

The book of Ruth is rich with good news for men and boys who are living in "the Century of Women."

Saving Boaz

According to traditional interpretations, when Boaz sets foot in the story, readers breathe a sigh of relief and exchange knowing glances. We have met the hero. Let the romance begin! His arrival awakens hope that Ruth's fortunes are about to change for the better. It isn't uncommon to hear contemporary single women say, "I'm waiting for my Boaz."

But relegating Boaz to a romantic figure not only downsizes him and cheats him of the enormous credit he actually deserves; it also distracts us from the truly powerful role he takes and the deep gospel wisdom his story contains. For far too long, we've been cheating Boaz by caricaturing him as "the guy who gets the girl."

Furthermore, that portrayal raises grave questions about his character. What kind of egregious abuse of power is involved when the owner of the field eyes a female gleaner with romantic motives? How will he dishonor his family by bringing home a bride who lacks social or economic advantages and, worse, is barren?

Besides, if Boaz had marriage in mind, what was the hold-up? Why didn't he at least send her home with his assurance that neither she nor Naomi would ever have to worry about hunger again? Instead, Ruth continues slaving in the hot sun for the entire harvest season.

In fairness to Boaz, the dissonance between the romantic version and the narrator's portrayal of a man *hayil* surely means Boaz deserves a closer look.

We learn he is an older man of Naomi's generation when he addresses Ruth as "my daughter" (2:8; 3:10, 11), just as Naomi addresses her (1:11, 12, 13; 2:2, 8, 22; 3:1, 16, 18). The genealogy at the end of the story reveals Boaz is Israel's native son, born to a prominent family in the leading tribe of Judah. His grandfather Nahshon was the commanding general of the tribe of Judah and the third man in rank after Moses and Aaron. Through Obed, the son Boaz fathers by Ruth, Boaz becomes the great-grandfather of King David, the royal line that ultimately leads to Jesus. Talk about pedigree!

At their first meeting, Ruth knows nothing about the landowner in whose field she comes to glean. So her proposals to this daunting older landowner included a high degree of apprehension. International Justice Mission engages countless legal battles globally to counteract the abuse of widows when tribal strongmen seize their property, depriving widows of their only means of sustaining their families.[5] That scenario plays over repeatedly in today's world. It was the kind of danger Ruth faced.

The Pivotal Moment

Much is made about the initial encounter between Ruth and Boaz in Boaz's barley field. Without question this meeting is *the* pivotal moment in the story. But no one could know ahead of time that things would turn out well. Good stories have tension. One of the key questions posed by the presence of Boaz is, how will this impressive man use his power and privilege?

For starters, the enormous social and cultural disparity between them could not be more pronounced. They are polar opposites. He holds all the advantages. The disadvantages belong to Ruth. Throughout human history and right up to the present, the differences between them are the makings of some of the most horrific violations of human rights. Only consider the explosive combinations: male and female, rich and poor, young and old, Jew and gentile, native-born and immigrant, powerful and powerless, valued and discarded. Anyone watching this nitroglycerin mixture would be expecting something terrible to happen, especially when her request implies criticism of how he's managing his field.

But Boaz's response to her request to glean in territory that was off-limits to gleaners is a show-stopper. He was not offended, although obviously taken aback. Her perspective on Mosaic law was eye-opening to him. Not only does he listen and grant her request, but he exceeds it with evident determination that nothing must prevent her from succeeding. He even serves her a meal. How countercultural is that?!

We must not miss the earthshaking implications of his response. Boaz has just been introduced as a man who needs no improvement. In the eyes of the culture (and also of the narrator) he is golden. And yet, his exchanges with Ruth are eye-opening to him. He realizes what she is trying to do. Her perspective sheds new light on a business he has been running for years.

It is one thing for notable theologians such as John Calvin or Jerome to engage in conversation with noble women who are wealthy patrons. It is quite another for a man of Boaz's stature to engage in conversation with a woman who culturally speaking is beneath him. He is bridging a cavernous gap. Yet, as the story demonstrates, and as he acknowledges, she is in every sense his match. The way he honors her bears that out and goes against the way life typically works in this world.

What if Boaz had dismissed, ignored, rebuked, or even abused her for violating social boundaries? How would the rest of the story have played out? Ruth and Naomi would have lived a hand-to-mouth existence. Naomi would not have revived. It never would have entered her mind to send Ruth to Boaz in hopes of finding shelter. Ruth wouldn't have attempted to rescue the legacy of Elimelech. His land would have remained fallow until later—perhaps after Naomi's death. The elders and villagers wouldn't have witnessed this stellar man becoming even greater by making unrequired, extraordinary sacrifices for Elimelech's sake. There would be no marriage and no Obed.

Boaz's response raises a huge issue for Christians. One of the biggest obstacles to a deepening walk with God is resistance to rethinking our beliefs, listening to others, learning, and changing. All through the Bible, God is repeatedly asking some of the people who walked with him the longest to be willing to be wrong and to learn and grow. Sometimes walking with God means learning truth that requires rethinking your entire life. Abraham's journey with God began in earnest when he was seventy-five—an age when people have a right to be settled in their ways. Abraham had to change, and with each change he grew deeper in his faith. More recently, after decades of ministry, a pastor began to realize he had gotten some things wrong. When one of his parishioners questioned what was happening, the pastor replied, "You gotta give me room to grow." Room to grow and the courage to change—that reflects what happened to Boaz.

Boaz openly violates cultural expectations in his interactions with Ruth. Instead of showcasing patriarchal standards of masculinity, Boaz subverts them. He bucks the system. He is not held captive to dominant definitions of masculinity. He is free of such expectations and big enough to do the right thing, even when it costs him. In his interactions with this foreign newcomer, Boaz accepts her influence and in doing so discovers room to grow.

Boaz was a man ahead of his time. In the workplace today, equal pay for women remains an unmet goal. Boaz went beyond equality. So Ruth's take-home pay was as much as fifteen to thirty times what a male harvester would pocket for a day of labor. Boaz pursued the spirit of God's law—to seek justice for the poor and to feed them.

Boaz and the Power of Power

When it came to the obligations of the kinsman-redeemer and levirate laws, Boaz enjoys loopholes that would make a defense attorney salivate. He isn't Elimelech's nearest relative, nor is he Elimelech's blood brother. Legally, he is beyond the demands of the law. Furthermore, Ruth's combination of the two laws is highly irregular, especially in Naomi's case, where the statute of limitations had expired. So when Boaz goes to Bethlehem to press the nearer kinsman-redeemer to purchase land he is likely to inherit anyway and to marry Ruth to produce a male heir for Elimelech, he's pressing his case beyond the requirements of the law. It raises the question, how did Boaz get away with this?

Boaz's self-appointed advocacy for Naomi on Ruth's behalf demonstrates how radically out of step he is with his culture. At the male-dominated seat of government, Boaz gives women legal voice. He assumes Naomi has property rights and insists that purchasing her land is an urgent matter. If that wasn't surprise enough, he bends the law to require the kinsman-redeemer to fulfill the levirate law too in lieu of a blood brother.

> **POWER CHOICES**
>
> "Power comes with hard choices whether a man acknowledges this or not. On the one hand, he can wield these powers for himself and his growing estate in such a manner that his own power in Bethlehem increases. On the other hand, he can take a countercultural stance and use his powers to empower and look out for the powerless and vulnerable. ... The challenge for Boaz will always concern how he will exert his powers and what he will do with the blessings Yahweh entrusts to him." ("The Power of Power," in Carolyn Custis James, *Malestrom: Manhood Swept into the Currents of a Changing World* [Grand Rapids: Zondervan, 2015], 119–20)

He also bends the law emphatically toward women's rights—a concept unheard of in ancient times but a pressing contemporary global issue today. And Boaz, a heavyweight among Bethlehem leaders, proves unstoppable. Not only does he push through everything Ruth requested, he depletes his own estate to rescue Elimelech, just as he vowed he would. The fact that not one man attempts to oppose him signifies just how powerful Boaz was.

Boaz shows how male power and privilege can become a powerful force for good. He voluntarily makes extraordinary sacrifices beyond what the law requires. But that's what *hesed* looks like.

His story also refutes the misguided adage that the rise of women comes at a cost for men. The rise of Ruth influenced Boaz to become a better man—one of the best men in all of Scripture.

Dead, Buried, but Not Forgotten

One of the beautiful surprises in the book of Ruth is that, contrary to initial impressions, not only Elimelech but also his two sons, Mahlon and Kilion, remain in the story from beginning to end. They appear in every chapter, even though all three are dead and buried. Battles are engaged, and the story moves forward to rescue *their* legacy—their land and lineage.

Their deaths precipitate Naomi's spiritual crisis. Their absence leaves her "empty." When Ruth delivers an astonishing load of winnowed barley, Naomi draws a firm straight line between this propitious turn of events and the husband and sons she is grieving. She exclaims that YHWH has not forgotten his *hesed* both "to the living *and the dead*" (2:20, emphasis added)—a reference to Elimelech and their sons. It is a remarkably hope-filled statement that reshapes how we think about loved ones we have lost. Those who have died still matter—not merely to those who grieve their loss but also to YHWH, who continues to show them *hesed* and act on their behalf. He doesn't forget them, their concerns, or their prayers.

Then, at the threshing floor, Ruth risks everything to rescue the dying line of Elimelech. She appeals to the levirate law to replace her dead husband, Mahlon, with a son. In the end, YHWH "enabled her to conceive," a son is born, and Naomi's empty arms hold the infant Obed. Elimelech's land will *not* be passed on to his unnamed nearest kinsman or even to Boaz. Instead, Obed will stand in for Mahlon and inherit Elimelech's land.

According to the genealogy that comes at the end of the book (4:18–22), Obed's son, Jesse, is the father of King David. Later, when YHWH sends Samuel to Bethlehem to anoint David as king, the land that Jesse and his sons occupy once belonged to Elimelech (1 Sam 16:1–13).

The Blessed Alliance

The book of Ruth dismantles the notion that the rise of women comes at a cost for men. In this ancient story there is a rare convergence where the efforts of women are furthered by their alliance with a man. Despite how the culture views women, YHWH regards them as indispensible to his purposes, and their actions, when shaped by YHWH's *hesed*, benefit the men.

In every encounter, Boaz isn't just being nice to Ruth and giving in to pressure. He actually *learns* from her. She brings a perspective to every conversation that is different from his. Their relationship points back to the beginning of time, when God created his male and female image bearers to represent him and do his work in the world together. God *blessed* the relationship between male and female—not only in marriage but in every male/female collaboration.

The Creator underscores the strategic importance of strong relationships between men and women when he says, "It is not good for the man to be alone. I will make an *ezer kenegdo* for him." *Ezer* is a Hebrew noun that in the Bible always appears in a military context and is recognized as a military term.[6] Considering the challenges the first man and woman faced and that a deadly Enemy was plotting an attack, it shouldn't surprise us that YHWH would use a military word to describe the female.[7] *Kenegdo* is another important Hebrew word that indicates the woman is the man's full partner. She is not his inferior or his superior. She is his match.[8]

Together, Ruth and Boaz give us a powerful example of the Blessed Alliance that God intended from the beginning. Together they accomplished more than either of them would have alone. In fact, alone they would have accomplished next to nothing insofar as Naomi and her family were concerned.

Boaz discovers through Ruth that there is more to living out his calling as YHWH's son than he has yet grasped. Her openness in reinterpreting Mosaic law makes Boaz a better man. His alliance with Ruth empowers her desolate mother-in-law's revival, blesses the men in their family, and ultimately proves strategic in advancing God's purposes for the world. By the end of the story, Boaz stands a whole lot taller than when he was first introduced.

The rise of women in this story also means Elimelech's legacy lives on in Obed. The book of Ruth proves the point. "It is not good for the man to be alone" (Gen 2:18). The point being that men actually need their sisters to step up and answer God's call on their lives. And we will yet see how indispensible Naomi is to YHWH's purposes for the world.

SUGGESTED READING

- ☐ Ruth 1:1–5; 4:16–22
- ☐ 2 Samuel 23:3–4

Reflection

Why is the book of Ruth often regarded as a good study for women but not also for men?

How does the book of Ruth dismantle the notion that if women take the lead in the story it comes at a cost for men?

How does Boaz model a gospel use of power for the flourishing of others?

How does the masculinity Boaz embodies clash with how our culture and even the church defines men?

___

___

___

9

BETTER THAN SEVEN SONS

"Sad stories do not have happy endings. ... [but] sad stories may yield new beginnings."[1] The words of biblical scholar Phyllis Trible ring true when it comes to the book of Ruth. Without question, the book of Ruth is undeniably a sad story. Recognized as a female Job, the bereft Naomi anchors grief and troubling questions about God at the center of the story. Her story is a gift to the church, for her honesty with God invites us to own our doubts, ask the hard questions, and engage honestly with God too.

Furthermore, it is important to reiterate that grief would always shape the landscape of Naomi's life. We are delusional to imagine that those whose lives are marked by deep tragedy will somehow, someday escape the weight of grief. Sandy Hook and Gold Star parents will go to their graves in grief, no matter how many good things happen to them after their losses.

No doubt Naomi went to her grave in sorrow over the husband and sons she buried in Moab. Like anyone who suffers the loss of a loved one, she would have been vulnerable to those unexpected, debilitating waves of grief that wash over a person with the slightest provocation. It only takes a whiff of memory, a well-intentioned but no less hurtful word spoken in ignorance, returning to a place once shared together, or other people's family photos of happy perfection. Sometimes the force of grief can ambush a person without any logical explanation. We are only kidding ourselves to imagine the story that began with Naomi's piercing cries of lament and anger against YHWH could end with all unhappiness erased.

However, even though the book of Ruth is fraught with heartache, it is also full of new beginnings, including one of the unlikeliest recorded in Scripture. For although Naomi is engulfed in sorrow and convinced her life is over, her daughter-in-law's bold advocacy awakens her to the active presence of YHWH's *hesed* on her behalf. From that awakening, a new hope springs forth from the ashes of Naomi's losses and shattered life. Ironically, Naomi's new beginning is deeply rooted in her suffering.

Naomi's experience echoes what grieving Yale professor Nicholas Wolterstorff wrote in the aftermath of his son's tragic death in a mountain climbing accident. "The world has a hole in it now. I shall look at the world through tears. Perhaps I shall see things that dry-eyed I could not see."[2]

From start to finish, the book of Ruth is ultimately YHWH's story. The whole story shifts into high gear when Naomi gains a clearer understanding of YHWH precisely because she looked at the world through tears. From something as mundane as a load of winnowed barley (something that would have passed unnoticed in better days), Naomi detected to her astonishment hard evidence of YHWH's unending *hesed* for her.

YHWH's love is not fickle—ebbing and flowing depending on the worthiness or performance of his child. Strange as it seems, circumstances are not a reliable indicator of YHWH's *hesed*. That earthshaking discovery refuted her belief that YHWH was against her. It also flew in the face of the patriarchal culture's definition of Naomi as a washed-up piece of driftwood—a cultural zero who had outlived her usefulness.

THE BIBLE'S REVOLUTIONARY VIEW OF WOMEN

"Throwing out a baby girl to die on the dung heap or burning a widow on her husband's funeral pyre are among some of the most appalling value statements the world has ever made about women. Negative statements about women run from these extreme atrocities to milder, more polite forms. But they all belong to the same fallen value system. The Bible's view of women rejects that entire system and introduces a whole new way of thinking. God's views of his daughters and his large vision for their roles in his kingdom are on a collision course with the world's view of women, and that collision is showcased in the book of Ruth." (Carolyn Custis James, *The Gospel of Ruth: Loving God Enough to Break the Rules* [Grand Rapids: Zondervan, 2008], 200)

Like Job, Naomi was forever marked by her losses. But the Naomi we see after that eye-opening moment is not the same woman who earlier despaired of God, of life, and of the future. No longer is she taking signals from the culture. Once she operates from the security of YHWH's *hesed*, she turns outward to think of Ruth and in the process becomes a collaborator and an active agent in advancing God's rescue operation for the world. Despite how hopeless life appeared when she was at her lowest, YHWH never abandons or discards his daughters or his sons.

From Zero to Better than Seven

The contrast between Naomi and Ruth could not be more striking. To be sure, they shared negative similarities. Both were widows. Neither had sons. Together they were both stranded as defenseless widows in a patriarchal culture. Both lacked the single most valued attribute in a woman: the ability to reproduce. After ten years of marriage without even a daughter to show for it, Ruth could not conceal her barrenness. The dismal zero ranking was glaringly emblazoned on her as condemningly as the infamous embroidered scarlet "A" that Nathaniel Hawthorne's Hester Prynne was sentenced to wear on her dress.

But Ruth's cultural ranking drops below zero when she migrates to Bethlehem with Naomi. Now on top of everything else, she is an immigrant, an outsider, a new convert with a pagan background, and she is scavenging to survive. Furthermore, she is disconnected from her past—she is rootless. Within patriarchy, the relationship that established a solitary young woman's identity and stature was that she was "the daughter of" so-and-so. When Boaz inquires, "Whose young woman is that?" he is looking to situate her on the social ladder. The answer, by itself, is a detriment. "She is the Moabite who came back from Moab with Naomi" (2:6).

In Israelite culture Ruth is a nonentity. But her ranking will quickly change. The place on the road between Moab and Bethlehem where Ruth dug in her heels and embraced Naomi, her people, and her God marks the turning point for Ruth—the new beginning of her story. After that moment, everything changed.

Her radical and defiant decision to stick with her mother-in-law did not go unnoticed in Bethlehem. Evidently, Naomi was talking, and so were her neighbors. Suddenly Bethlehemites begin discarding the cultural yardstick for women as they begin to admire a woman for deeper reasons than the men in her life or the number of her sons. Instead, they value her for how she lives before the face of YHWH. Against the backdrop of Ruth's cultural deficiencies, a whole new value system emerges that ultimately aligns with what Naomi also learns about herself.

Boaz's first words to Ruth reveal early signs of his esteem, for her reputation has preceded her. "I have been told all about what you have done for your mother-in-law since the death of your husband—how you left your father and mother and your homeland and came to live with a people you did not know before" (2:11). He continues by praying YHWH will shower her with blessings and by acknowledging that she has taken refuge under YHWH's wings—a prayer he will ultimately participate in fulfilling.

Further interactions with her, the fresh, eye-opening perspective she brings to Mosaic law, and her bold, relentless advocacy for Naomi only heighten his esteem for her. At the threshing floor, his admiration for her skyrockets as she puts herself at risk, despite years of barrenness, in hopes of conceiving a male heir for Naomi and Elimelech. Clearly, Boaz has been observing her conduct throughout the harvest season.

Her conduct was impeccable, her mission undistracted. She never veered from her determination to care for Naomi to focus on herself. His response is filled with respect and praise as he employs strong language (the same language used to describe him in 2:1) to describe the character and courage of this remarkable young foreigner.

> The LORD bless you, my daughter. This kindness is greater than that which you showed earlier: You have not run after the younger men, whether rich or poor. And now, my daughter, don't be afraid. I will do for you all you ask. All the people of my town known that you are a woman of noble [*hayil*] character. (3:10–11)

She brings a perspective to Mosaic law that too often is missing, for she speaks as one whom the law is designed to protect and bless—the hungry, the poor, the widow, the foreigner, the oppressed. How easy it is from the safe security of power and privilege to read God's law or to draw conclusions from the life of Jesus that won't cost us so much. How would our understanding break open if we listened to those whom the law and Jesus' teaching are intended to shield, relieve, and prosper?

Ruth shocks Boaz, and she will shock us too. She will expose and break through a settled contentment with "good enough" to walk with God into uncharted territory. And she will lead Naomi and Boaz to join her in a better story.

The elevation of Ruth spills over into the community when Boaz purchases Naomi's land and claims

Ruth, the widow of Mahlon, as his wife "to maintain the name of the dead with his property, so that his name will not disappear from among his family or from his hometown" (4:10).

Now the city elders and villagers chime in with words of inclusion for this immigrant from Moab. These are the people Ruth embraced before she arrived in Bethlehem. Now they are embracing her. They link her to some of Israel's most prominent matriarchs—mothers of the nation and of the tribe.

> Then the elders and all the people at the gate said, "We are witnesses. May the LORD make the woman who is coming into your home *like Rachel and Leah*, who together built up the family of Israel. ... Through the offspring the LORD gives you by this young woman, may your family be like that of Perez, *whom Tamar bore* to Judah." (4:11–12, emphasis added)

Like Rachel and Leah, Ruth is a nation builder, as the epilogue of her story documents (4:18–22). Like Tamar, Ruth sacrificed and took enormous risks to recover the legacy of her dead husband (two dead husbands in Tamar's case).

The community's statement of inclusion surpasses issuing a green card or granting citizenship to an immigrant. Before anyone knows how this story will turn out, whether or not Ruth's barrenness will persist or her union with Boaz will only produce daughters, the community publicly embraces Ruth as *one of them*.

Yet even this doesn't end the lengths to which Ruth will go for Naomi. Nor does it complete the strong value statements the book of Ruth is making regarding women.

God Bless the Child

Then YHWH "enabled [Ruth] to conceive, and she gave birth to a son" (4:13). Obed's birth is celebrated, but not in the way we might expect. A chorus of women encircles Naomi with blessings that celebrate YHWH's goodness to Naomi and that climax Ruth's elevation. They also reveal the surprise ending to the story—not that Boaz, Ruth, and Obed make the perfect family, with Naomi as Obed's doting grandmother or the baby's nanny. "Then Naomi took the child in her arms and cared for him" (4:16). The story concludes with the widow who tragically lost her two sons in the beginning, cradling Obed in her arms. The women rejoice, "Naomi has a son!" (4:17). As Robert Hubbard writes,

> The author viewed [Naomi] more as a "mother" than a mere guardian. ... Ruth's unusual action was one last gift to Naomi, the gift of a son to care for as her own—a son to replace the deceased ones, a son who would later reciprocate her care as she grew old. ... Legally, the child was already Elimelech's heir and hence Naomi's son.[3]

Ruth makes the ultimate *hesed* sacrifice. By giving her son to Naomi, Ruth reverses Naomi's emptiness.

The explanation that sums up all that YHWH has done for Naomi also comes from the women who employ the most coveted accolade for any woman in the ancient patriarchal world. "For your daughter-in-law, who loves you and who is *better to you than seven sons*, has given him birth" (4:15, emphasis added).

This is no cliché. According to the women, Naomi is actually better off with Ruth than women who had given birth to what was regarded as the perfect number of sons.

> Older women counted on their sons to care for them, to protect them from exploitation and the harsh elements of society, to be their voice, to stand up for their rights, and to preserve their father's name and estate by bringing the next generation of male descendants into the world. Ruth did all of those things for Naomi at great cost to herself and in a culture that tied her hands behind her back, denied her a voice, refused her access to the legal system, and regarded her as useless. It was all uphill for Ruth. But she did it anyway. Not even seven sons would have done as much.[4]

But the story doesn't stop here. The genealogy that concludes the book of Ruth moves the story into the future. Unbeknown to Ruth, Naomi, and Boaz, cosmic issues are afoot. YHWH is advancing his purposes for the world through the hard choices and selfless actions they are making to address a local family crisis. The genealogy at the end informs us that the family line Ruth and Boaz were rescuing was the royal line of King David that ultimately leads to Jesus.

The birth of Obed marks a new beginning for Naomi. Who is qualified to raise the grandfather of the future king? Who possesses the wisdom that this young child will need to pass on to future generations?

Instead of discarding Naomi, YHWH is redeploying her for a crucial kingdom mission, and Naomi is ready. She will draw on wisdom carved into her soul in the school of suffering and in the dark night of the soul that followed.

From Naomi, Obed will learn lessons of *hesed*. He will hear her story. He will learn of her losses, doubts, anger, despair, and of the day she discovered that YHWH's *hesed* never stops. From her perspective, she is simply raising a little boy. In reality she is raising the grandfather of Israel's future king.

The wisdom Obed gains from Naomi will take deep root, and he will pass on lessons of YHWH's *hesed* to his son Jesse, who will pass this wisdom on to his son David. King David will pass that truth on to us when he writes of YHWH, "Surely your goodness and *hesed* will follow me all the days of my life" (Ps 23:6).

From the mother who gave him birth, Obed will learn about bold, courageous, risk-taking faith and the sacrifices it compels. That same brand of faith will show up in his grandson, who, armed only with five smooth stones and a shepherd's sling, will defeat a giant Philistine warrior.

From his father, Obed will discover both in word and deed a different, not-of-this-world kingdom brand of masculinity that rejects what the patriarchal culture will teach him and that Jesus ultimately will embody. He will learn that power and privilege come with responsibility and that these are gifts, not entitlements, that can be used for unimaginable good or unspeakable evil.

Who knew the book of Ruth was so countercultural? Who knew it contains some of the strongest affirmations of God's love for *both* his daughters and his sons and how much we matter to him—even those the world despises and devalues, even when we've lost our way, even when we die and are buried? The book affirms and honors women and men beyond any cultural value system. This ancient story challenges us to rise up to live self-consciously before the face of God and to truly love him in more radical, rule-breaking ways that convey God's *hesed* to others in life-renewing ways.

So this harmless looking little story is actually not soothing, but is instead subversive—not merely to the world of Naomi, Ruth, and Boaz but to our world too. It compels us to reexamine how our own cultural and religious values reflect a fallen world's social systems and to compare our relationships with the relationships we witness in this story. The book of Ruth raises the bar for all of us and ultimately means all of us need to change.

From our twenty-first-century perspective, it's hard to ignore the fact that the genealogy at the end of the book of Ruth is pointing us to Jesus. The story summons us to ponder the powerful examples of Ruth, Boaz, and Naomi, how God transforms each of them, and how the three of them become a Blessed Alliance that causes all three to flourish as God's image bearers and invests their selfless actions with global significance that lives on well beyond anything they ever knew or imagined.

But the book of Ruth also beckons us to look beyond this remarkable trio to Jesus the perfect *imago Dei*, to make him our study, and to imitate him. What did

Jesus mean when he said, "My kingdom is not of this world"? How is his kingdom on a collision course with our own culture, and how does it challenge what we as Christians can so easily settle for in our own lives as "good enough"? If we make Jesus our focus and begin to embrace his heart for this world, we'll begin to act in *hesed* ways in our closest relationships, with our Christian brothers and sisters, our neighbors, colleagues, and with people who are different from us. And when that happens, the world will know that Jesus has come and that his kingdom is not of this world.

SUGGESTED READING

- ☐ Ruth 4:13–17
- ☐ Psalm 23 (esp. v. 6, "mercy" = *hesed*)
- ☐ John 17:20–23

Reflection

How does Naomi's true value overthrow how the culture valued her and how she valued herself?

___

___

___

Why do the women regard Ruth as "better than seven sons"?

___

___

How does God's view of his daughters transform their value and how indispensible they are to advancing his purposes in the world?

To get a sense of the strength of the Blessed Alliance in this story, how would the story play out if Naomi, Ruth, or Boaz weren't in it? How would that change the story for the other two?

How does the book of Ruth challenge how you see yourself and how necessary other men and women are to how you fulfill God's calling on your life?

RECOMMENDED READING

Campbell, Edward F., Jr. *Ruth*. Garden City, NY: Doubleday, 1975.

Davis, Ellen F., and Margaret Adams Parker. *Who Are You, My Daughter?—Reading Ruth through Image and Text*. Louisville: Westminster John Knox, 2003.

Hubbard, Robert J., Jr. *The Book of Ruth*. New International Commentary on the Old Testament. Grand Rapids: Eerdmans, 1988.

James, Carolyn Custis. *The Gospel of Ruth: Loving God Enough to Break the Rules*. Grand Rapids: Zondervan, 2008.

———. *Half the Church: Recapturing God's Global Vision for Women*. Grand Rapids: Zondervan, 2011.

———. *Malestrom: Manhood Swept into the Currents of a Changing World*. Grand Rapids: Zondervan, 2015.

LeCocque, André. *Ruth: A Continental Commentary*. Translated by K. C. Hanson. Minneapolis: Augsburg Fortress, 2004.

Sakenfeld, Katharine Doob. *Ruth*. Interpretation: A Bible Commentary for Teaching and Preaching. Louisville: John Knox, 1999.

NOTES

Chapter 1: Introduction

1. See Robert J. Hubbard Jr., *The Book of Ruth*, New International Commentary on the Old Testament (Grand Rapids: Eerdmans, 1988); André LeCocque, *Ruth: A Continental Commentary*, trans. K. C. Hanson (Minneapolis: Augsburg Fortress, 2004); Carolyn Custis James, *The Gospel of Ruth: Loving God Enough to Break the Rules* (Grand Rapids: Zondervan, 2008).

2. To read more, see Carolyn Custis James, *Half the Church: Recapturing God's Global Vision for Women* (Grand Rapids: Zondervan, 2011); *Malestrom: Manhood Swept into the Currents of a Changing World* (Grand Rapids: Zondervan, 2015); and *Gospel of Ruth* (Grand Rapids: Zondervan, 2011).

3. To read more, see James, *Malestrom.*

4. See David Beldman, *Deserting the King: The Book of Judges* (Bellingham, WA: Lexham Press, 2017).

Chapter 2: Entering the World of Naomi and Ruth

1. See "When a Food Security Crisis Becomes a Famine," *UN News Centre*, July 21, 2011, www.un.org/apps/news/story.asp?NewsID=39113#.WL8jDRiZNxg.

2. Bonnie Bowman Thurston, *The Widows: A Women's Ministry in the Early Church* (Minneapolis: Fortress, 1989), 25. Commenting on Luke 7:11–17, Thurston writes, "When Jesus raises this man from the dead, he is in fact restoring two persons to life in the community: the man and his mother."

3. Nicholas D. Kristof and Sheryl WuDunn, *Half the Sky: Turning Oppression into Opportunity for Women Worldwide* (New York: Knopf, 2009), xvii.

Chapter 3: Inconsolable

1. Anne Barnard and Karam Shoumali, "Image of Drowned Syrian, Aylan Kurdi, 3, Brings Migrant Crisis into Focus," *New*

York Times, September 3, 2015, www.nytimes.com/2015/09/04/world/europe/syria-boy-drowning.html.

2. William Dalrymple, "The Outcasts," *The Sunday Times Magazine*, August 16, 1992, 24.

3. Also, in the gospels, women are readily identified as widows without explanation (Luke 7:12; Mark 12:41–44). This practice is still maintained in full-fledged patriarchal cultures today.

4. The story of Judah and Tamar (Gen 38) centers on levirate practices.

5. "If brothers are living together and one of them dies without a son, his widow must not marry outside the family. Her husband's brother shall take her and marry her and fulfill the duty of a brother-in-law to her. The first son she bears shall carry on the name of the dead brother so that his name will not be blotted out from Israel" (Deut 25:5–6).

6. Mayo Clinic Staff, "Infertility—Symptoms and Causes," *Mayo Clinic*, www.mayoclinic.org/diseases-conditions/infertility/symptoms-causes/dxc-20228738 (accessed September 14, 2017).

Chapter 4: Undocumented!

1."Push and Pull Factors of International Migration," study conducted by the Netherlands Interdisciplinary Demographic Institute (NIDI) and Eurostat, the statistical bureau of the European Union's Commission of the European Communities International, commissioned to study the push and pull factors that determine international migration flows. The study commenced in 1994 and concluded in 2002. https://web.archive.org/web/20061010035808fw_/http://www.nidi.knaw.nl/web/html/pushpull/index.html (accessed September 14, 2017).

2. John Clifton, "150 Million Adults Worldwide Would Migrate to the USA," *Gallup*, April 20, 2012, www.gallup.com/poll/153992/150-Million-Adults-Worldwide-Migrate.aspx.

3. Robert L. Hubbard Jr., *The Book of Ruth*, New International Commentary on the Old Testament (Grand Rapids: Eerdmans, 1988), 114.

4. Hubbard, *Book of Ruth*, 119. Hubbard explains, "The vague *Thus* reflects the formula's ultimate origin in ceremonies which solemnized ancient treaties and covenants. As the oath was pronounced, symbolic actions (cf., e.g., the modern gesture of

slashing one's finger across the throat) alluded to the slaughter of animals, an earlier part of the ceremony, and invoked a similar fate for breach of promise by the speaker. Thus, Ruth voluntarily took on dire, unspecified consequences if the conditions next stipulated happened. Given Naomi's testimony against Yahweh (v. 13; cf. vv. 20–21), Ruth could conceivably expect the worst."

Chapter 5: The Power of *Hesed*

1."C. S. Lewis on Writing," *Letters of Note*, April 3, 2012, www.lettersofnote.com/2012/04/c-s-lewis-on-writing.html.

2. Miles Custis, "*Chesed*," in *Faithlife Study Bible* (Bellingham, WA: Lexham Press, 2012, 2016).

3. Carolyn Custis James, *The Gospel of Ruth: Loving God Enough to Break the Rules* (Grand Rapids: Zondervan, 2008), 115.

4. Christopher J. H. Wright, *Old Testament Ethics for the People of God* (Downers Grove, IL: InterVarsity, 2004), 168.

5. Robert L. Hubbard Jr., *The Book of Ruth*, New International Commentary on the Old Testament (Grand Rapids: Eerdmans, 1988), 138.

6. André LaCocque, *Ruth*, trans. K. C. Hanson (Minneapolis: Fortress, 2004), 63.

7. Hubbard, *Book of Ruth*, 73.

8. R. Laird Harris, Gleason L. Archer Jr., and Bruce K. Waltke, eds., *Theological Wordbook of the Old Testament* (Chicago: Moody Press, 1980), 1:271–72.

9. LaCocque, *Ruth*, 65.

Chapter 6: *Restless* in Bethlehem

1. Genesis 38:26 is often translated, "She is more righteous than I." But further examination of the text by Hebrew experts has led to a more accurate translation: "She is righteous; I am not." Judah's collision with Tamar in this moment is a turning point for him. It halts his spiritual nosedive. When he learns Tamar is pregnant from prostitution, he orders an honor killing for a crime he has committed. When she presents him with his seal, cord, and staff, Judah is compelled to look in the mirror. This is the moment that the prodigal comes to his senses. The Judah who appears after this encounter is a radically changed man. It is one of the most powerful chapters in all of Genesis. See

also "The Father Wound," in Carolyn Custis James, *Malestrom—Manhood Swept into the Currents of a Changing World* (Grand Rapids: Zondervan, 2015), 77–94.

2. Although this matter is debated, the evidence on balance clearly suggests what we would define as rape. Richard M. Davidson presents a compelling argument for defining David's actions as rape in his article "Did King David Rape Bathsheba? A Case Study in Narrative Theology," *Journal of the Adventist Theological Society* 17, no. 2 (Autumn 2006): 81–95. At the popular level, Professor David T. Lamb agrees, "David Was a Rapist, Abraham Was a Sex Trafficker: What We Miss When We Downgrade Old Testament Abuse Stories to Sexual Peccadillos," *Christianity Today*, October 22, 2015. In *King David: A Biography* (Oxford: Oxford University Press, 2000), 157, Stephen L. McKenzie states that Bathsheba "is presented as the passive victim of [David's] lust." In Walter Brueggemann's *1 and 2 Samuel*, Interpretation: A Bible Commentary for Teaching and Preaching (Louisville: John Knox, 2012), 273, he supports the notion that David's actions were violent and dehumanizing: "The verbs rush as the passion of David rushed. He sent; he took; he lay (v. 4). The royal deed of self-indulgence does not take very long. There is no adornment to the action. The woman then gets some verbs: she returned, she conceived. The action is so stark. There is nothing but action. There is no conversation. There is no hint of caring, of affection, of love—only lust. David does not call her by name, does not even speak to her. At the end of the encounter she is only 'the woman' (v. 5). The verb that finally counts is 'conceived.' But the telling verb is 'he took her.' "

3. Albert the Great (Albertus Magnus), *Quaestiones Super de Animalibus* in *Opera Omnia*, ed. Auguste Borgnet (Paris: Apud Ludovicum Vives, 1890–1899), book XV, quest. 11.

4. Robert L. Hubbard Jr., *The Book of Ruth*, New International Commentary on the Old Testament (Grand Rapids: Eerdmans, 1988), 201.

5. Hubbard, *Book of Ruth*, 203. "As is well known, the term 'feet' could be used as a euphemism for sexual organs. ... Though not demonstrable as a euphemism here, it may have been chosen to add to the scene's sexual overtones. In any case, 'place of feet' meant the place where his feet lay."

6. Geraldine Brooks, *Nine Parts of Desire: The Hidden World of Islamic Women* (New York: Anchor, 1996), 67.

7. Frederick Bush, *Ruth/Esther*, Word Biblical Commentary 9 (Waco, TX: Word, 1996), 222. Bush writes regarding levirate marriage: "The marriage is effected by its consummation; no ceremony is necessary."

8. "If any of your Israelite relatives go bankrupt and are forced to sell some inherited land, then a close relative, a kinsman redeemer, may buy it back for them" (Lev 25:25 NLT).

9. "If brothers are living together and one of them dies without a son, his widow must not marry outside the family. Her husband's brother shall take her and marry her and fulfill the duty of a brother-in-law to her. The first son she bears shall carry on the name of the dead brother so that his name will not be blotted out from Israel." (Deuteronomy 25:5–6).

10. "While Naomi clearly did not have Levirate marriage in mind, but believed that option didn't exist (cf. Ruth 1:11–13), she seems to have expected Ruth to return to her a married woman. Her question, upon Ruth's return home in the morning, 'How did it go?' seems to imply that expectation. This fits also with the irregularities of this marriage arrangement: no formal marriage negotiations and no bride price or dowry. There will be no fanfare or marriage celebration. He can take her now, or not. The fact that legal issues become involved and someone exists who has first rights to Elimelech's estate than Boaz throw a wrench in Naomi's plan and cause Boaz to exercise restraint." Carolyn Custis James, *The Gospel of Ruth: Loving God Enough to Break the Rules* (Grand Rapids: Zondervan, 2008), 219.

Chapter 7: Breaking the Rules for Naomi

1. Carolyn Custis James, *The Gospel of Ruth: Loving God Enough to Break the Rules* (Grand Rapids: Zondervan, 2008), 178. "In ancient times, the city gate was not only the point of entry into town and the most logical place to look for fellow villagers coming and going, it was also the heart of the community. The gate was the seat of government and the site of important business transactions a platform for local dignitaries, a pulpit for prophetic messages, and the hub of local gossip for the entire village."

2. The question comes up as to why Naomi sent Ruth to Boaz, if Elimelech had a nearer kinsman. Did Naomi make a mistake and send her daughter-in-law to the wrong man? The mix-up makes it clear that Ruth and Naomi were at cross purposes, for Naomi certainly knew Boaz wasn't Elimelech's nearest relative. If Naomi intended to address the legal issues Ruth raised surrounding her deceased husband, she never would have sent her to Boaz. But Naomi was merely looking for mercy and hoped that Boaz's kindness to her daughter-in-law would dispose him to understand her concerns for Ruth's safety and be gracious.

3. At this point the narrator explains a tradition that men during the time of Boaz followed to formalize the sale of land. "Now in earlier times in Israel, for the redemption and transfer of property to become final, one party took off his sandal and gave it to the other" (4:7). And so the nearer kinsman removed his sandal.

The initial readers were living *at least* three or four generations later, during the reign of David or Solomon. Already this ritual for ratifying the transfer of property from one man to another had fallen out of practice and needed explaining. It requires even more explaining today. Some have suggested it could have had something to do with YHWH's instruction to Abraham to "Go, walk through the length and breadth of the land, for I am giving it to you" (Gen 13:17). But no one knows for certain. We are even further removed from this tradition and are left to guess at the significance of a sandal.

Chapter 8: The Manly Side of the Story

1. Tom Brokaw, "Welcome to the Century of Women," April 29, 2013, http://leanin.org/discussions/welcome-to-the-century-of-women/.

2. Hannah Rosin, *The End of Men: And the Rise of Women* (New York: Riverhead, 2012), 10.

3. Rosin, *End of Men*, 13.

4. Leon Morris, *Ruth: An Introduction and Commentary* (Downers Grove, IL: InterVarsity, 1968), 250.

5. See www.ijm.org.

6. See "Eve—A Forgotten Legacy," in Carolyn Custis James, *Lost Women of the Bible: The Women We Thought We Knew* (Grand Rapids: Zondervan, 2005), 27–45, and "The *Ezer* Unbound," in

Carolyn Custis James, *Half the Church: Recapturing God's Global Vision for Women* (Grand Rapids: Zondervan, 2011), 99–118.

7. Robert Alter notes that *ezer kenegdo* "connotes active intervention on behalf of someone, *especially in military contexts*, as often in Psalms" (emphasis added). Robert Alter, *Genesis—Translation and Commentary* (New York: Norton, 1996), 9.

8. "The man no doubt recognized the animals which were brought to him as helps, but they were *not counterparts of equal rank*. So God moved on, in the most mysterious way, to create the woman—from the man! As distinct from the animals, she was *a complete counterpart* which the man at once recognized and greeted as such" (emphasis added). Gerhard von Rad, *Old Testament Theology: The Theology of Israel's Historic Traditions* (New York: Harper & Row, 1962), 1:149–50.

Chapter 9: Better than Seven Sons

1. Phyllis Trible, *Texts of Terror: Literary-Feminist Readings of Biblical Literature* (Minneapolis: Fortress, 1984), 2.

2. Nicholas Wolterstorff, *Lament for a Son* (Grand Rapids: Eerdmans, 1987), 26.

3. Robert L. Hubbard Jr., *The Book of Ruth*, New International Commentary on the Old Testament (Grand Rapids: Eerdmans, 1988), 264.

4. Carolyn Custis James, *The Gospel of Ruth: Loving God Enough to Break the Rules* (Grand Rapids: Zondervan, 2008), 203.